Regulating Social Work

A PRIMER ON LICENSING PRACTICE

ANTHONY A. BIBUS III

and

NEEDHA BOUTTÉ-QUEEN

LYCEUM
BOOKS, INC.

Chicago, Illinois

© 2011 by Lyceum Books, Inc.

Published by
LYCEUM BOOKS, INC.
5758 S. Blackstone Avenue
Chicago, Illinois 60637
773–643–1903 fax
773–643–1902 phone
lyceum@lyceumbooks.com
www.lyceumbooks.com

6   5   4   3   2   1   11   12   13   14

ISBN 978-1-933478-91-3

Printed in Canada.

Library of Congress Cataloging-in-Publication Data

Bibus, Anthony.
Regulating social work: A primer on licensing practice /
Anthony A. Bibus III and Needha Boutté-Queen.
p.   cm.
Includes bibliographical references and index.
ISBN 978-1-933478-91-3 (pbk. : alk. paper)
1. Social workers—Licenses—United States.   2. Social workers—Licenses.
I. Boutté-Queen, Needha.   II. Title.
KF3721.B53   2011
344.7303'13—dc22
2010011823

Contents

List of Figures and Tables

Figures

Tables

Acknowledgments and Dedication

With deep gratitude, we would like to thank the many whose expertise has benefited us, including Augsburg College student worker Jenna Forbrook, Augsburg College librarian Mary Lee McLaughlin, and education professor Vicki Olson; faculty and staff colleagues at Texas Southern University, Augsburg College, and the Center for Global Education; Association of Social Work Board (ASWB) colleagues, especially Troy Elliot and Kathleen Hoffman; staff and board members from Texas and Minnesota chapters of National Association of Social Workers (NASW) and the Texas and Minnesota boards of social work, especially Minnesota Board Executive Director Kate Zacher-Pate; Lyceum staff and reviewers, in particular Prof. Thomas Meenaghan; Jose Luna, Prof. Kim-Anne Perkins, and Center for Global Education staff in Cuernavaca; James Trelstad Porter for Spanish translation; our loving proofreading spouses; and contributors Malcolm Payne, Monit Cheung, Chathapuram Ramanathan, and Subhabrata Dutta. Without their astute and informed input, constructive and creative suggestions, apt comments, and cogent advice, this primer would be less useful. The book represents our best effort to incorporate this help in coming to our judgments, conclusions, and recommendations. Any mistakes are our own.

We dedicate this book to our parents.

Notes on Authors and Contributors

Authors

Anthony Bibus

Anthony Bibus is professor in the Social Work Department at Augsburg College, Minneapolis, Minnesota, where he has taught in both the BSW and MSW programs since 1992. After five years as BSW director, he served as department chair for a decade. He is a licensed independent social worker. In addition to teaching, his practice background includes four years as a juvenile probation counselor, four years as a child protection and family-based services worker, and eight years as a social services supervisor. Tony is a graduate of the doctoral program at the University of Minnesota School of Social Work (1992). From 2000 to 2008, he served as a professional member of the Minnesota Board of Social Work. During this service, he led several legislative committees and task forces engaged in developing and implementing a comprehensive revision of the social work practice act in Minnesota and a variety of other regulatory policies. He also participated in revising the Association of Social Work Board's Model Social Work Practice Act as a member of the Discipline and Regulatory Standards Committee. In addition to a major report for the board of social work on licensing exemptions, his publications include articles and chapters in the areas of field education, supervision, cultural competence, child welfare, family-based services, international social work, welfare reform, and work with involuntary clients.

Needha Boutté-Queen

Needha Boutté-Queen is associate professor in the Social Work Department at Texas Southern University in Houston, Texas, where she has served on faculty and as department chair since 2006. Needha's background includes working with the Lutheran Social Services of Kansas and

Oklahoma Emergency Foster Care and Quality Assurance Programs, the Illinois Facility Fund, Depelchin Children's Center Resource and Grants Management Department, and Spaulding for Children (Houston). Her dissertation, "Identifying Barriers to Obtaining Social Work Licensure," was developed as a result of barriers she faced as she moved between the states of Illinois, Oklahoma, and Texas following her graduation from the University of Chicago School of Social Service Administration in 1995.

Contributors

Monit Cheung, MA, MSW, PhD, LCSW

Monit Cheung is professor at the Graduate College of Social Work, University of Houston. She is principal investigator of the Child Welfare Education Project, a state partnership program funded federally by Title IV-E for training child welfare social workers, and associate director of the Child and Family Center for Innovative Research. She has been a social worker for thirty-four years; she is a licensed clinical social worker specializing in play therapy, family counseling, child/adolescent counseling, child protection, sexual and domestic violence, and incest survivor treatment. She has practiced as a volunteer clinician by providing counseling and case consultation at the Asian American Family Services, and she served as a consultant trainer for the Hong Kong Social Welfare Department and the Hong Kong Police Force. Using an experiential and practice-oriented approach, Cheung has taught at the graduate level for twenty-three years. She has presented 202 papers in workshops or conferences and written 386 articles, books, book chapters, and research reports on child protection and parenting issues in English and Chinese. Her research interests are related to treatment effectiveness in areas of child sexual abuse, creative family therapy, therapeutic touch, and immigrant adjustment. Cheung currently serves on the Diocesan Review Board for the Protection of Children and Young People at the Diocese of Galveston–Houston, advisory board member of Catholic Charities and Asian American Family Services, and the board of the End Child Sexual Abuse Foundation in Hong Kong.

Subhabrata Dutta, PhD, MPhil, PGCRM, MSW

Subhabrata Dutta has worked as an associate professor in the Department of Social Work, Assam University (A Central University), Silchar, India, since 2004. Dutta started his academic career as a faculty member at

Tata Institute of Social Sciences, Mumbai, and taught two years there. He has published two books: he is the author of *Democratic Decentralization and Grassroot Leadership in India* (2009) and is coauthor of *Women Speak* (2008). He has contributed ten refereed articles and eleven research papers in Indian and international journals and as editorial page pieces in India's leading newspapers. His major areas of interest, practice, and scholarship focus are social work, governance and social development, gender issues, and child protection. Dutta has visited many European countries, including the Netherlands, Germany, Austria, Poland, Slovenia, and Malaysia to present papers at seminars and symposiums and for other academic and research purposes.

Malcolm Payne, BA, DipSS, PhD

Malcolm Payne is adviser in the Policy and Development Department at St. Christopher's Hospice, London, where he has provided creative and complementary therapies, day care, mental health care, social work, and spiritual care. He has broad experience of social work, having worked in probation; social work, particularly with people who are mentally ill; and in management in social service departments. Payne was head of Applied Community Studies, Manchester Metropolitan University, for many years, during which he was chair for four years of the Association of Professors of Social Work; during that time, he also was involved in child and mental health service advisory projects and research. Now emeritus professor there, he also is honorary professor at Kingston University/St. George's Medical School, and docent in social work at the University of Helsinki, Finland. He has been extensively involved in international social work, leading and working on projects to develop social work and social policy in China, Russia, and the countries of eastern Europe. He has lectured and presented papers all over the world on social work education, theory and practice, teamwork, and palliative care. Together with Norwegian social work academic Gurid Aga Askeland and others, he has published a number of articles about the impact of globalization and postmodern ideas on social work. His other publications include ten books and some 250 shorter works in thirteen languages. Recently, together with colleagues at St. Christopher's Hospice, he has been researching and publishing in the fields of social work, welfare rights, day care, and other aspects of palliative care services.

Chathapuram Ramanathan, PhD, ACSW, LMSW, CAC

Chathapuram Ramanathan has worked in the human service area for three decades. Ramanathan graduated with a master's and a doctoral degree from the University of Illinois. His practice and scholarship focus is on addiction recovery, cross-cultural issues, social development, and clinical social work. Ramanathan has been providing psychotherapy services for over twenty years, and he is a licensed marriage and family therapist. He has taught full-time in the graduate schools of social work for more than ten years. He has published approximately twenty refereed articles and is the coauthor of *All Our Futures* (1999); he is also coauthor of *Human Behavior in a Just World: Reaching for Common Ground*, scheduled for release in 2010. In the late 1980s and early 1990s, Ramanathan served on the Michigan Governor's Multicultural Mental Health Education Task Force. He was a member of the Council on Social Work Education's (CSWE's) International Commission from 1992 to 2004. He has been a trained site visitor for more than fifteen years, reviewing graduate and undergraduate programs for accreditation. In addition to serving on several agencies' boards, Ramanathan has been an alternate member of NASW's National Ethics Committee since 2007. He serves on the editorial boards of two major journals: *Drugs and Society* and *Social Development Issues*. Ramanathan has presented more than fifty papers and workshops in Brazil, Canada, Germany, Hong Kong, India, Ireland, Malaysia, the Netherlands, Poland, Portugal, South Africa, Sri Lanka, Thailand, Turkey, the United Kingdom, and the United States.

Preface

Imagine that you are a young parent, alone with your first child. No matter what you try, the three-month-old infant will not stop crying. The baby's other parent is away and no other caring adult is close; you are exhausted and desperate for the baby to stop crying and go to sleep so you can get some rest. When you take the infant in your arms, you find yourself squeezing its chest to stop the wailing. Perhaps you throw the baby down on a bed, or worse. And you remember the crisis center near your neighborhood and the ad you've seen by the center prompting parents at their wits' end to call and talk to a social worker. Or when you take your baby to its next health-care checkup, the nurse notices a bruise on the child's arm and makes an abuse report to child protective services, and the social worker visits you.

You are this parent, now meeting the social worker for the first time, either because you sought her out voluntarily or because he was assigned to you as the result of an involuntary referral. So much would depend on whether you could trust and rely on the competence of that social worker. Questions race through your mind: "Will the social worker respect me and understand me and my situation? Will the social worker know how to help me? Will the social worker keep my child safe? How do I know that the social worker is qualified to help me?"

In the United States, you would presume that the social worker was licensed because most other helping professionals—nurses, doctors, and psychologists—are licensed. And chances are that the social worker is licensed: in many states, but not all, social workers must be licensed.

So, fate steps in to determine whether or not the social worker assigned to help you is licensed. That is, if the social worker is licensed, you could have some assurance that the social worker has achieved minimum levels of education, training, knowledge, and skills, and that in addition to these competencies the social worker has made a commitment, manifested by maintaining a license to practice, to abide by a set of professional stan-dards. If the social worker's competencies or actions fall below these stan-dards, you would have recourse to report the incompetence, unethical practice, or malfeasance to an independent board that is sanctioned by law to investigate, order compliance or discipline, and seek appropriate redress for the client, the baby, the family, and the general public. If the social worker is not licensed, there is less recourse.

This is not to say that you have little chance of receiving adequate ser-vices from an unlicensed practitioner. In fact, it could be that a social worker without a license might be as well educated, trained, and competent as a licensed counterpart—or even more so. Even if the social worker is not licensed, you might have access to appeals and other protections offered by supervisory and administrative auspices within the agency providing services. However, if the social worker is not licensed you would not have the independent licensing board to turn to should unethical practice occur. Nor would an unlicensed social worker have the same degree of support and encouragement to maintain professional integrity and competence as a licensee. Thus, when the issue is client protection, it should not be a flip of the coin that determines whether the social worker assigned to a client (who, after all, could be one of us or one of our loved ones) is licensed. Conversely, licensure is not foolproof. Indeed, the primary goal of this book is to prepare readers to identify areas of improvement in regulation of social work practice and to develop the knowledge and skills needed to mobilize with others and influence needed changes in licensing policies so that those who use social work services have the best chance possible of successful work. Young parents, children, the elderly, and all people in vulnerable conditions or circumstances deserve no less.

For regulators, [Kryzanek said], the little guy is the person to be kept in mind when decisions about licensure and discipline have to be made. Everyone is the "little guy" some time in their lives. . . . Recently, Kryzanek said, he has been the "little guy," searching for advice, care and treatment for his wife, Sue. Sue Kryzanek died in October after five months in a "system" that included not only medical people but social workers. . . .

He found it supportive and comforting that someone was saying for each professional caregiver, "You can trust that if we gave them a license, they can do the job. And if they are incompetent or unethical you can come to us with a complaint and we will listen and respond."

Source: "Now about the little guy . . . ." (2007). This article featured the outgoing president of the Association of Social Work Boards, Roger Kryzanek.

Introduction

This primer on regulation of social work practice serves as a guide for social work students on their journey toward becoming professional licensed practitioners. Like medicine, law, and psychology, social work is a regulated profession in the United States. The authors are social workers and social work educators who have consulted and conducted research with licensing boards and the Association of Social Work Boards (ASWB), a nonprofit member-governed association of social work licensing boards. Realizing that the path to licensure may appear murky and even daunting at times, we strive to provide clear reference points as well as a framework for analysis to sort through the twists and turns of regulatory policies and processes and the complex controversial issues that interweave with social work licensing. We start with explaining the purpose of licensing and outlining the typical steps students take to become licensed to practice social work in the United States.

Purpose of Licensing

As we will discuss in more detail in chapter 1, the most rigorous form of regulation of social work practitioners is licensure. In the United States, states are authorized to regulate professions such as social work; there is no federal or national license for any profession. While all fifty states now regulate social work practice, a few still rely on the less-rigorous certification or registration rather than full-fledged licensing (Randall & DeAngelis, 2008). The primary purpose of social work licensing is to establish in statute a set of legally enforceable minimum standards to which social work licensees are held accountable. These standards specify the required educational qualifications, examination scores, and competencies that applicants must demonstrate when they apply for a license; in addition, the standards encode the professional practice activities and ethical conduct expected of licensees.

In many states in the United States, the law that incorporates licensing standards is called a "practice act." The practice act authorizes a board to enforce these standards and to investigate and respond to reports that a licensee's credentials or practices have not met the minimum standards or that an individual is practicing social work without a license. If the report is substantiated, licensing boards take corrective or disciplinary action to bring the social worker's practice back into compliance, if possible. Depending on the need to protect the public, boards can reprimand or fine licensees, impose conditions on or restrict their practice, require education or supervision to improve their practice, and, in extreme cases, suspend and revoke their licenses. (See ASWB, 2007b, 2010c; and Jost, 1997 for overviews of boards' typical composition and powers.)

People who use social work services provided by social work licensees thus have some assurance of the competence of their social workers and legal recourse to address unlicensed, unlawful, lapsed, impaired, improper, incompetent, unprofessional, unsafe, or unethical practices. In short, the purpose of social work licensing is often stated simply: to protect the public.

In order to provide effective protection for those who use social work services, legislation usually restricts the title of "social worker" to persons who are licensed as social workers. This function of social work regulation is referred to as "title protection." It is often the first step states take in regulating social workers before moving to adopt a practice act, which more fully protects the public by regulating social workers' professional actions as well as their professional title.

A model social work practice act is available through the Association of Social Work Boards (ASWB; www.aswb.org). This publication serves as a guide to member boards in developing or amending licensing legislation in their jurisdictions. Section 103 of this model act states the purpose of social work licensing this way:

> It is the purpose of this Act to promote, preserve, and protect the public health, safety, and welfare by and through the effective control and regulation of the practice of social work; the licensure of social workers; the licensure, control and regulation of persons, in or out of this state that practice social work within this state.

As we will discuss later in this primer (see chapter 4: Social Work Profession(al)-in-Environment: SW-PIE), there are other secondary purposes and side effects of licensing, not all of them necessarily congruent with the mission of social work. For example, licensure could be considered as a benefit to the profession of social work itself and a distraction from its "particular attention to the needs and empowerment of people who are vulnerable, oppressed, and living in poverty" (NASW, 2008, preamble). Some opponents of licensure have criticized proponents for being mainly interested in securing the livelihood of social workers instead of protecting the clients. Critics argue that licensing can be a means to advance the credibility and status of practitioners of the licensed profession in comparison to other professions with which they compete for clientele and thus can be a barrier to interdisciplinary collaboration. Because the services of licensed professions are often listed in legislation and policies as eligible for payment from public funds (e.g., Medicare and Medicaid in the United States) or insurance, advocates of licensure may focus much of their attention on sustaining third-party reimbursement for social work services. In addition, licensure can restrict the size or composition of a workforce by designating only those with certain qualifications as eligible for the license. For example, in social work this dynamic has been experienced as excluding practitioners of color or practitioners for whom English is a second learned language; this dynamic thus can be discriminatory. Some professional social work associations, such as the National Association of Black Social Workers, have at times opposed some licensing initiatives, claiming that licensure does not serve clients as much as serve the social workers themselves. On balance, however, lawmakers in every state have deemed it to be in the public interest to regulate social workers in order to protect residents of their states.

Steps to a Social Work License

To become eligible for a social work license, students (and other applicants) in most states and other jurisdictions in the United States must first earn a bachelor's degree in social work (BSW) or master's degree in social work (MSW) from an academic program accredited by the CSWE. Some states do not license BSW practitioners and allow only MSW graduates to apply for a social work license. This is one illustration of the need for students to keep in mind that in the United States there is no national license for social workers: each of the state and territorial boards of social work in the United States (and those in the Canadian provinces) has a separate distinct set of legislation, rules, policies, and procedures. Although the steps toward licensure are similar across the country, there are variations in particulars, such as whether students can apply to take the license examination before graduating. So, before embarking on the journey toward licensure, students first should contact the board that regulates social work in the state (or in other jurisdictions such as Washington, DC, or Puerto Rico) where they plan to practice. (See ASWB's [2007b, 2010c] guide comparing states' licensing laws and regulations and ASWB's website.)

In addition to supplying identifying information, background, experience, and work history and submitting to criminal background checks, applicants also provide educational information and arrange for official transcripts to be sent to the board. Importantly, the application usually also requires answers to a series of personal history questions such as these:

> "Have you ever been disciplined, sanctioned, or found to have violated a code of ethics or conduct?"
>
> "Have you ever been refused or denied admission to a social work program?"
>
> "Have you ever withdrawn from any educational program while subject to disciplinary action, or have you been dropped, suspended, placed on probation, expelled, fined, sanctioned or requested to resign from any educational program because of alleged misconduct?"

(See Federation of Associations of Regulatory Boards, 2001, p. 5.)

Applicants supply explanations or affidavits when they answer any question in the affirmative; it should be noted, though, that answering the questions affirmatively does not automatically disqualify an applicant. Applicants must be scrupulously honest or risk charges of perjury and possibly their future career in social work.

Although some states allow students in good standing to begin the process of applying for their license a few months before actually graduating so that they can complete the application, submit to required background checks, pay the various fees entailed, and take the examination, graduates cannot begin practicing as a social worker until they have been licensed (unless their practice qualifies for an exemption). Thus, the second step in the licensing process, the license examination, may be completed in the same period as completion of the degree program, or shortly afterwards. All jurisdictions in the United States but one (California) have selected ASWB's standardized examination as their test to ensure that applicants have the minimum competencies for licensed practice. ASWB has developed a number of examinations, each of which is updated regularly based on a job analysis, that is, surveys and other research of actual social work practice. Passing either the bachelor's or master's examination is required for initial licensure.

Once the application process is completed and all other requirements are satisfied, applicants receive their license. In some states, this means the new licensee must begin by practicing under supervision of a licensed social worker. In these cases, typically, at least two years of full-time supervised practice is required before the licensee is authorized to practice without formally approved licensing supervision. In other states, the new social worker is not required to meet this criterion unless the licensee intends to attain a clinical or specialized license. In addition, in most states licensees must complete a specified number of continuing education hours during each renewal period and attest to compliance with licensing rules or submit other documentation, as well as pay their renewal license fee. These fees in most states fund either partially or totally the operations of the licensing boards that set the standards for licensure.

After two years of authorized supervised practice and continuing education, in many jurisdictions MSW licensees may become eligible to take the examination for an advanced practice license, such as Licensed Independent Clinical Social Worker (LICSW) or Licensed Clinical Social Worker (LCSW). By this time, most licensees are familiar with and accustomed to the licensing process. Therefore, we will not devote as much attention in this primer to this stage in the process (except as it relates to the controversies discussed later).

In summary, there are essentially three steps to obtaining an initial license to practice social work followed by one or two more steps to independent practice (Figure 1.1). First, earn a social work degree (BSW or MSW) from an accredited institution; second, apply for a social work license and prepare to take the licensing examination; and third, pass the examination. In some jurisdictions, additional steps include completing at least two years of supervised practice. If interested in a license to practice at an advanced level, licensees maintain continuing education, abide by standards of practice and ethics, and meet other supervisory and renewal requirements to be eligible for the next step: taking and passing the advanced level examination.

FIGURE 1.1 STEPS TOWARD LICENSE

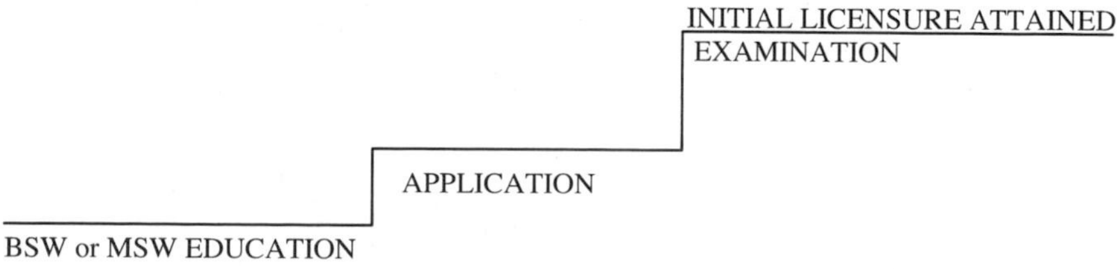

INITIAL LICENSURE ATTAINED
EXAMINATION

APPLICATION

BSW or MSW EDUCATION

Social Work: A Career, a Profession, a Vocation

For many social work students and licensees, and for the authors of this primer, licensing is more than a series of steps. It can reinforce our identity within the profession of social work. We have enjoyed fulfilling careers in social work, both with and without licensure, but social work can be even more meaningful than a career or a profession. It can be a calling and, in the deepest sense, our vocation.

We join social worker and author Malcolm Payne in thinking about social work as central to our identity. In his book *What Is Professional Social Work?* (2007a), Payne reflects on a lifelong career in social work, and on his international connections and extensive record of publications on social work theory and philosophy. His insight is that social workers, their clients, and society coconstruct social work as they interrelate. Social workers show the social work process in our interpersonal work, which in turn is valued by other professionals and service users. . . . Social work's complexity, which is difficult to put in a nutshell, is nevertheless its strength, and it is "unique in its particular combination of the social and the psychological with its values and objectives" (p. 189):

> Looking across different countries, therefore, we can identify a variety of different social works, with a range of roles. However, we can also identify continuities, and these continuities lie in the claim to connect the interpersonal with the social and the social with the interpersonal. (p. 175)

We invite students to consider what role licensing plays in the formation of social work's identity and to reflect with us on the meaning of social work as a regulated profession in our lives. In the concluding chapter, we will share our reflections.

Outline for the Primer

This primer is a guide, then, not only to the process of becoming a licensed professional, but also, potentially, to a lifetime of meaningful work. Hence, its chapters cover the range and depth of social work licensure in as comprehensive a fashion as is possible for a brief primer. Chapter 1 reviews the historical development of social work licensure. Chapters 2, 3, and 4 present the current landscape of social work licensure, providing students with a framework for analysis of legal issues, glimpses into regulation of social work globally, and opportunities to think through the complex and interrelated controversies surrounding licensure. The concluding chapter reflects on the role of regulation in the social work profession, highlighting, for example, the roles played by professional associations and educational programs as distinct from licensing boards. It ends with suggestions for discussion questions and class assignments. Finally, appendix A proposes learning activities and discussion questions, and appendix B suggests resources for students to continue learning about their profession. We welcome correspondence, questions, corrections, and suggestions (especially regarding resources on licensing).

CHAPTER ONE

Historical Background

SOCIAL WORK IN THE UNITED STATES has not always been a regulated profession. While social work was growing into a distinct profession here during the late nineteenth century and early years of the twentieth century, other already-established professions, such as medicine, dentistry, and law, experienced development of formal public regulation and licensure. According to social historian Walter Trattner, by the late 1800s professionals such as "teachers, engineers, geologists, chemists, political scientists, and so on" had been identified as meeting criteria for being considered members of a profession (Trattner, 1999, p. 233). That is, each of these professions had established its own body of knowledge, its specific and unique set of skills learned through higher education and training, and an identity and set of values subscribed to by members of the profession.

Citing Shimberg (1985) in their survey of the historical development of professional social work credentialing, Thyer and Biggerstaff note that "by the early 1900s a dozen occupations had achieved licensed status" (1989, p. 5). According to economics professors Law and Kim (2005), "by the mid-twentieth century, there were more than 1,200 state occupational licensing statutes, averaging twenty-five per state, for at least seventy-five occupations ranging from physicians to embalmers" (pp. 725–726). Physicians were regulated in every state by 1900, teachers by 1930, and attorneys and dentists by 1940 (p. 730, Table 1).

Other relatively new professions that often are allied with social work, such as psychology, successfully pursued licensed status across the country before social work. By 1977, fifteen years before all states in the United States regulated social work, every state licensed psychologists (Reaves, 2006). Meanwhile, whether social work is yet fully a profession is still argued today; regulation of social work practice has been a topic of discourse, debate, and some controversy since at least 1920 (Thyer & Biggerstaff, 1989, citing Arne, 1952). This chapter provides a brief overview of how social work became a licensed practice and of what we know about the impact of licensure on the quality of services.

Samuel Goldsmith's paper presented to the National Conference of Social Work in Minneapolis in 1931 is an example of an early discussion of the need for social work practitioners to have an equivalent set of requirements for professional preparation and registration, certification or licensing similar to other professions (i.e., surgery, nursing, dentistry, law, accounting, architecture, veterinary medicine, and teaching). Goldsmith was the executive director of Jewish Charities of Chicago at the time and was reflecting on the maturation of social work as a profession across the United States. He observed that regulation of older professions, such as medicine, had been evolving from requiring no specialized formal training to requiring at least two years of premedical college training.

Referring to social work as a "peripatetic profession" (Goldsmith, 1931, p. 556), Goldsmith explained that each state establishes its own set of requirements but also recognizes the common standard elements of professional preparation in order to employ workers from other states. In chapter 2 and chapter 4 we will visit in more detail the somewhat fragmented picture of contemporary social work regulation in the United States (ASWB, 2007b, 2010c; Boutté-Queen, 2003; DeAngelis, 2000, 2001; Randall & DeAngelis, 2008; Robb, 2004).

As we will see in chapter 4, many of today's debates about licensing social workers echo the dilemmas and arguments Goldsmith addressed. While acknowledging that social work regulation was in an earlier stage of development than were some other professions, perhaps because "the practice of social work is almost exclusively under auspices of groups that represent the public and presumably safeguard the public" (Goldsmith, 1931, p. 555), Goldsmith concluded that regulation of social workers is important and desirable for protecting the interests of people "who are, or may become, the objects of the application of the techniques of social work":

> It is undoubtedly true in our profession, as it is true in other professions, that the percentage of error and the concomitant ineffectiveness, if not more serious results of poor work, will be large so long as it may not be possible to restrict the practice of social work to those who have the skill and (or) the training to conduct the various practices involved, in an able manner. (pp. 560–561)

Discussions about the value of social workers being licensed did not evolve into formal legislative proposals and lobbying efforts until near the end of World War II, when California legislation established registration of social workers there in 1945. (In Puerto Rico, regulation of social work practice began earlier, in 1934, but most other jurisdictions did not follow suit until decades later; for more detail, see the timeline of statutory credentialing in Table 1 in Thyer and Biggerstaff, 1989, pp. 14–18; see also ASWB, 2007b, 2010c.)

Remarking that "social work lagged behind many other professions, even those much younger and less well established," Barker and Branson (2000, p. 184), explain that up through the 1950s in the United States licensing was presumed not to be needed because the services primarily were provided by social workers under the auspices of social agencies, and were not typically provided by individual practitioners in private practice. As a result, clients could rely on bureaucratic oversight and careful supervisors to ensure ethically sound service delivery. "It was believed that the supervisors could do everything needed" (p. 185). Gradually, however, it became clear to NASW members and other social workers that the protections afforded clients by recourse to supervisors and agency appeal processes were not adequate. Nor was voluntary commitment to NASW's *Code of Ethics* enough to assure the public that all social workers were properly trained and would abide by minimum standards.

The criticism that licensing was self-serving and would set up an elitist class of social workers was prominent in early debates (as it is today). During the 1970s, though, the drive for professional recognition, the need for access to reimbursement for mental health services, and the desire to afford clients better legal protections led social workers in every state to move toward licensure. According to Barker and Branson (2000), "the one consistency in all states is that the purpose of social work licensing statutes is not to protect the social worker or the social work profession but to protect the consumer from social workers" (p. 193). Although substantially variable in scope of practice or title governed, by 1992 all fifty states plus the District of Columbia, Virgin Islands, and pioneering Puerto Rico had legislation regulating social workers' practice (Randall & DeAngelis, 2008). In addition, by 2008 ten provinces of Canada were regulating social work practice.

What We Know About the Impact of Licensing on Quality of Services

Given this long history of discussion and the attention that licensing receives at U.S. social work conferences and in government policies (see, for example, historical reviews by Biggerstaff, 1995; Garcia, 1990a; Hard-castle, 1977; Randall & DeAngelis, 2008; Thyer & Biggerstaff, 1989), one might anticipate that there would be a robust and extensive literature on social work licensing. However, there are fewer published articles on social work licensing than expected. Thyer and Biggerstaff's 1989 monograph provides an annotated bibliography of 128 out of 199 citations covering social work regulation, vendorship, and private practice, but their review has not been replicated in a generation. Publications that are more recent include general descriptive essays such as encyclopedia entries by Bigger-staff (1995) and Randall and DeAngelis (2008), journal articles such as Hoffman's (2002), reviews of licensing controversies such as exchanges between Karls and Mathis (in Gambrill & Pruger, 1992), and Thyer's (2000) and Seidl's (2000) debate over whether social work educators should be licensed. A book-length presentation and critique of the state of clinical social work licensing in the United States with recommendations for improvements has been published recently (Groshong, 2009). A few theses and dissertations have focused on social work licensing (e.g., Boutté-Queen, 2003; Cloutier, 1997; Kinderknecht, 1995; Matz, 1996; McCarthy, 2008 [focusing on genetic counselors from disciplines including social work]; and Overson, 2005). There have been a handful of descriptive and empiri-cal studies conducted, such as those by Boland-Prom (2009), Daley and Doughty (2007), and Cavazos (2001); the latter remarked as well on the scarcity of licensure research (p. 72). Finally, some published articles have presented studies or critiques of the ASWB licensing examinations for social workers and have questioned their validity (Black & Whelley, 1999; Johnson & Huff, 1987, 1989; Marson, DeAngelis, & Mittal, 2010; Randall & Thyer, 1994; Thyer, 1994).

A variety of social work texts include only short passages, and not whole chapters, on licensing (e.g., Dubois & Miley, 1999, p. 104; Glicken, 2007, p. 60; Morales & Sheafor, 2001, p. 72; and Weinbach, 2005, pp. 36–37). A typical introductory text in social work programs (Farley, Smith, & Boyle, 2006) devotes less than a page to certification and licensing, most of it describing the development of NASW's certification process through its Academy of Certified Social Workers. The authors explain that "certifica-tion" is a term sometimes used interchangeably with "credentialing" and "licensing," but that technically it refers to authorization to practitioners from some authority (government body or professional association) to claim expertise in particular competencies and scopes of practice. Certifi-cation often reserves the right to use the title of the profession solely to certified individuals. "Registration" is a term that sometimes covers regula-tion only of the use of the title of "social worker" and sometimes also entails some of the requirements typical under licensure, such as account-ability to minimum standards of conduct (Pew Commission for the 21st Century, 1995, p. 2).

However, neither certification nor registration usually includes the full package of rigorous legal and regulatory functions included under licens-ing governed by practice acts. As Farley and colleagues (2006) explain, "*Licensure* is the term most frequently used and usually refers to authoriza-tion by a board to practice in the profession" (p. 404; italics in original). See box 1.1 for more elaboration from an international perspective of the distinctions between certification, registration, and licensing from contrib-utors to this primer.

Resource texts on social work and the law vary as well from no mention

---

BOX 1.1 CERTIFICATION, REGISTRATION, AND LICENSING

Subhabrata Dutta and Chathapuram Ramanathan, who describe the devel-opment of regulation of social work in India in chapter 3 of this primer, turn to Hickman (1994) for a clear explanation of the terms "licensing," "certification," and "registration," which often are used in interchangeable and thus confusing ways. Professional licensing, they write, means a state-required license to practice within a particular profession and is the state's best effort at protecting its citizens from professional misconduct and mal-practice. Licensing differs from certification or registration in that licens-ing usually has stringent requirements. It also offers greater status and, in many cases, the only route toward getting direct payment for the provision of certain professional services. Through licensing, the specific knowledge base of the profession is recognized by law to be unique. In the case of social work, the law requires all those who claim to engage in the practice of social work, as defined in the law, to hold a social work license. Some countries require social workers to be licensed, while usually making certi-fication and registration (whether offered by the state or by a professional organization) voluntary. Holding a license generally requires the licensee to adhere to a code of ethics or professional conduct. If this code is vio-lated, the license can be revoked or other disciplinary actions taken. The primary purpose of a license is to ensure quality control and thus protect the public.

Monit Cheung, who describes social work regulations in Asia in chapter 3 of this primer, clarifies further that licensure requirements are legally stated to safeguard title protection to protect the use of the title "social worker," and to ensure practice protection to protect the practice of social work with required standards and professional ethics.

of legal regulation of social work practice (Albert, 2000) to brief passages (Saltzman & Proch, 1990; and Schroeder, 1995) to chapters (Karger, 1988) and comprehensive explanations and analysis (Barker & Branson, 2000; see also Madden's presentations of the legal principles in social work practice, e.g., Madden, 2007). Social work licensing often over the years has appeared to be a relevant issue only for practitioners in private practice. The assumption was that clients of social workers in the public sector already have protections and procedures to redress grievances built into the government processes by way of elected officials' oversight as well as bureaucratic safeguards and due process rights.

Thus, social work licensing often has aimed to protect clients of private practitioners or clients of nonprofit or for-profit agencies, and has been viewed as less necessary or optional to protect clients of social workers in the public sector. Indeed, NASW's workforce study of licensed social workers indicates, "licensed social workers in many practice areas are most likely to work in the private/nonprofit sector (e.g., addictions, adolescents, aging, health and mental health)" (Center for Workforce Studies, 2006, p. 18). However, the same study found "social workers in some other practice areas are more likely to work for public sector agencies" such as child welfare, criminal justice, higher education, and school social work (p. 18; 28% of respondents to a survey updating this study practiced in public or government organizations: Whitaker, 2009, p. 19). Clients in these settings are often in very vulnerable conditions, frequently without options, resources, or freedom to seek help elsewhere, and sometimes are mandated to meet with the social worker. The question of whether these clients should have the same protections and recourses afforded to clients of licensed social workers in other settings is germane.

A recently published basic text, DiNitto and McNeece (2008) does devote some pages to licensing, explaining, "by specifying the knowledge and skills required for a given level of social work practice, and a common code of professional conduct, individual state boards use licensure to protect those using social work services" (p. 23). Citing one of the few dissertations on social work licensing (Kinderknecht, 1995), DiNitto and McNeece comment briefly on the gap in public protection resulting from exemptions. They offer some evidence suggesting that licensees exempted from passing the licensing examination may be more likely than licensees who have passed the examination to be named in complaints that their practice fell below ethical standards, and more likely to have those complaints substantiated. They conclude,

> In many states, the great majority of individuals holding positions that most people would describe as social work jobs do not hold a social work

degree. . . . It is possible that the reprofessionalization for social work could be achieved through the implementation of rigorous licensing laws and a licensing process that is not directed solely toward the practice of clinical social work. Society needs social workers who are well prepared in all areas of practice. (p. 383)

While agreeing that extending licensing regulation to social workers in all practice settings including public agencies and "eliminating exclusions to licensure may promote the identification of the social work profession with quality services offered in a variety of settings to people who are unable to obtain services from other sources" (p. 112), Biggerstaff (2000) cautions that legal regulation of service providers does not guarantee that those services will in fact turn out to be effective: "Effectiveness of services calls for at minimum practice based on sound research, on-going empirical validation of interventions, commitment to consistently updating practice knowledge and skills, critical skills in evaluating interventions, and skill in evaluating one's own practice effectiveness" (p. 114; see also the special issue in the *Journal of Social Work Education* on evidence-based practice and the editorial by Walker, Briggs, Koroloff, & Friesen, 2007). Moreover, as the next section demonstrates, we do not know enough yet from empirical research about what impact licensing has on the actual quality and helpfulness of services in the lives of people who use them.

Empirical Studies from Social Work on Impact of Licensing

The discourse on various aspects of social work licensure can be divided into four main sections: social work licensure history (Thyer & Biggerstaff, 1989), licensure attainment and sanctions (i.e., Biggerstaff, 1992; Borenzweig, 1977; Cherry, Rothman, & Skolnik, 1989; Johnson & Huff, 1987; Schwartz & Dattalo, 1990), topical discussions regarding professional aspects of licensure (i.e., Cavazos, 2001; Gray, 1990), and the impact of licensure on professional practice (i.e., Corazzini-Gomez, 2002; Pardeck, Chung, & Murphy, 1997; Scheyett et al., 2009; Simons, 2006; Teasley, Baffour, & Tyson, 2005).

With regard to the first two areas, the historical implementation of licensure is covered elsewhere in this primer, as are those issues related to license attainment and sanctions. However, literature in the area of professional issues is varied. For example, Cavazos (2001) utilizes survey responses from two sets of bachelor's-level graduates of a CSWE-accredited program to examine similarities and differences between those who are licensed and those who are not. Specifically, the author sought to obtain information on "the effects of licensure status on employment salary and the use of work titles" (p. 72). Graduates of the 1991 and 1996 graduating classes of the University of Texas–Pan American were approached via mail about their potential participation in this research project: twelve of the twenty-seven earlier graduates and forty-one of the forty-seven later graduates agreed to take part, for a total sample size of fifty-three.

Respondents were primarily female (89 percent) and of Mexican-American descent (87 percent); 79 percent were gainfully "employed in social work or social services positions" (Cavazos, 2001, p. 73). Cavazos reports that 42 percent (n = 17) of the forty-one later graduates did not take the licensing examination. "The absence of an employment-related requirement" and "cost" were the two most frequently cited reasons for not taking that examination. With regard to the same 1996 graduates, neither title nor licensure appeared to have had an impact on salary. Due to the small number of respondents from the 1991 graduating class, it was not possible to determine whether the same held true for this group. What did appear to be true for both groups was the presence of "social work related [sic] job titles, including case-worker, casemanager [sic], specialist, counselor, educator, liaison, and advocate" (p. 74), regardless of the presence or absence of licensure among respondents.

As has already been discussed, the terms used to describe regulation of the professional practice of social work often are used interchangeably. Moreover, research into the differences between those regulated at different levels is scant. With this in mind, Gray (1990) utilizes a "two-step process" to explore "the interplay of supervision and licensure" (p. 56) among respondents who were certified, registered, and nonlicensed. Out of the 900 potential respondents, 300 each from a state with registration, a state with certification, and a state that did not have licensure at the time of the study, 104 respondents who were receiving professional supervision were surveyed on their experiences. Findings indicated that, where licensure guidelines prevailed, supervision was more likely to last longer and occur with regular frequency.

When it comes to the impact of licensure on practice, the results are as varied as the topics explored. For example, an attempt to determine whether social work–educated license holders differed from their social work–licensed counterparts who were not educated as social workers utilized responses from 155 professionals for analysis, 97 of whom were both educated as social workers and licensed. In this study, Pardeck and colleagues (1997) find differences only in terms of political views and the absence of a social work education among nonwhite respondents.

However, in their exploration of this topic, the authors report "no statistically significant differences between the two groups in the areas of practice setting, practice behaviors and attitudes, and treatment modalities used in practice" (p. 151).

Though the Pardeck and colleagues' (1997) study finds no statistical differences between licensed social workers who were social work educated and those who were not with regard to practice modalities, the presence or absence of social work education instead of licensure itself was actually being measured as a variable. In contrast, other studies have examined licensure as a variable. In an effort to determine whether client characteristics influenced the allocation of agency resources, Corazzini-Gomez (2002) uses case vignette assessments with 355 Massachusetts case managers employed in elder services. After reading each case, the case manager was asked to assign services based on characteristics of the clients described. Each of the 355 respondents was to respond to six vignettes; responses for a total of 2,054 vignettes were received for a completion rate of approximately 96 percent. Demographic data indicated most respondents were female (89 percent) and white (91 percent), and approximately 81 (23 percent) were licensed social workers. In the final model of a five-model regression analysis, social work licensure was found to be significantly associated with the generosity of the case plan. Specifically, "when controlling for the differential effects of demeanor and attitude by social work licensure status, case managers licensed as social workers assessed more generous care plans" (Corazzini-Gomez, 2002, p. 748). In addition, findings indicated social workers were less likely to provide services that are more generous to those vignette clients who indicated they did not want help than they were to clients who indicated they wanted help. Likewise, when client descriptions indicated they were polite yet reluctant to discuss certain things, case managers who were also licensed social workers were less generous in terms of resource allocation. Pardeck and colleagues (1997) suggest that self-determination may play a role in both of these findings.

While there are other studies that have looked at the impact of licensure on social work practice, the reader must be cautious about drawing any conclusions regarding the effectiveness of licensure based on the findings of those completed to date. Studies of this nature are often hindered as a result of methodological shortcomings that include small or nonrepresentative samples, inconsistencies in technology, the absence of control groups, missing data regarding respondents' educational attainment, and the current inability to compare across states due to varying licensure levels.

Empirical Studies from Allied Disciplines on Impact of Licensing

Across other professions, the question also has been raised of what empirical evidence exists that licensure in fact results in improved quality of services. Might data gathered in studies of licensing beyond social work support the contention that a licensed social work workforce would result in broader protection of the public from practice that falls below minimum standards? The coauthor Bibus conducted a systematic search of the literature from allied health professions looking for recent studies that examined whether licensed practitioners' patients or clients received higher quality care than that provided by unlicensed practitioners.

The following is a summary of findings from reviews of studies across occupational licensing, followed by findings from studies in nursing, medicine, physical therapy, and teaching. Kleiner (2006) and others observe that there has not been "a randomized experiment of consumers going to unregulated versus regulated service providers" and comparing outcomes (p. 56). After reviewing major studies on the effects of licensing several occupations (including dentists, teachers, and optometrists, among others) from 1978 to 2005, he found that instead of experimental designs,

> most analyses of licensing . . . analyze more highly regulated regimes relative to less regulated ones. In these cases the results show that licensing has modest to no effects on the demand for the service or on the quality of service received by consumers. (p. 56)

To be sure, other reviews of studies have found some positive impact. For example, in their report to the Minnesota Board of Social Work, Alexander and Johnston (2008) state that their review of existing studies indicated that licensed individuals may be more likely to be involved in continuing educational and professional development, to show cultural sensitivity, and to develop longer-lasting relationships with clients. (See Law & Kim, 2005, for discussion of the link between licensing in medicine and reduced mortality rates historically in the United States from 1900 to 1930.)

Nevertheless, as will be evident when we review studies in the allied professions below, empirical research on the effect of licensing itself is scarce to nonexistent. Most of the studies reviewed below focused on certification and continuing education postlicensure.

NURSING SPECIALTY CERTIFICATION

In their article on specialty certification in licensing nurses, Briggs, Brown, Kesten, and Heath (2006) note that "the primary method of ensuring public safety is licensure" (p. 47). Defining certification as a process for validating "an individual's knowledge related to a specific area of practice" (p. 47), they cite a 2001 study demonstrating that nurses with recent certification report making fewer errors than the overall average:

> The link between certification and safety of patients is reinforced by the research finding that nurses who had been certified for 5 years or less reported that they made fewer errors in caring for patients than the overall group of certified nurses who responded reported. (Briggs et al., 2006, p. 48)

Their review of the literature found "scant and mixed" support for concluding that certification improves the quality of care beyond basic safety. However, they cite two reports that certified nurses performed at a higher level than noncertified nurses in some aspects of practice (for example, planning, collaborating, and evaluating). They recommend further research to confirm a link between safety, high-quality services, and certification.

Another recent review of the literature screened more than 700 studies to analyze seventeen papers reporting on peer-reviewed empirical research into the correlation between registered nurse staffing and the costs and lengths of stay in hospital for patients. The authors (Thungjaroenkul, Cummings, & Embleton, 2007) conclude, "replacing professional nurses with unlicensed assistive personnel is inappropriate to achieve cost-containment objectives" (p. 263). Instead, they recommend that to reduce patient mortality hospitals should increase the proportion of registered nurses.

PHYSICIAN SPECIALTY CERTIFICATION

In a systematic review of all relevant studies between 1966 and 1999 and of selected "well-conducted" studies since then, Sutherland and Leatherman (2008) found that the practice of physicians who are certified in a specialty tends to be of higher quality than the practice of noncertified physicians. One study in California found that the risk for disciplinary action being taken against noncertified physicians is greater than for those who are certified. Sutherland and Leatherman conclude, "The association between certified status and higher quality care is consistent across the range of clinical specialties, geographical locations, and permutations of applying and interpreting regulation" (p. 441).

A Canadian study found that scores on examinations for doctors did correlate years later with practice outcomes and patient care (the higher the scores, the better preventive care and disease management). "The most important findings of this study were that the relationships between certification examination scores were sustained through the first 4 to 7 years of practice" (Tamblyn et al., 2002, p. 3024).

These conclusions should be taken with some caution because there have been criticisms of the validity of several studies in this area (Grosch, 2006).

PHYSICAL THERAPY CONTINUING EDUCATION

One review of the literature (covering studies done before 2000) found "most studies reported in the medical literature show little relationship between participation in traditional CE [continuing education] and improved patient outcomes" (Vaughn, Rogers, & Freeman, 2006, p. 82). The Federation of State Boards of Physical Therapy is working to help state boards set up procedures for assuring consumers and the public that continuing education in fact leads to continuing competencies for practitioners (such as post–continuing education examinations, online discussions on how continuing education applies in practice, continuing education instructors mentoring participants in practice, and supervision.)

TEACHER CERTIFICATION AND LICENSING

A report from the National Research Council (NRC) of the National Academies summarizes the evidence so far on the impact of certification of teachers by the National Board of Professional Teaching Standards on student achievement (Hakel, Koenig, & Elliott, 2008; Ladd, Sass, & Harris, 2007). The council reviewed eleven studies in two states (Florida and North Carolina) that measured students' achievement, comparing results for students whose teachers had been certified to results for students whose teachers were not certified.

> Findings from these studies show that, in both states, students taught by board-certified teachers had higher achievement test gains than did those taught by nonboard-certified teachers, although the differences were small and varied by state. . . . We see a relationship between board certification and student achievement, although the relationship is not strong and is not consistent across contexts. (p. 7)

According to the NRC panel (quoted in Viadero & Honawar, 2008, p. 1), "Most of the studies asked: When students have nationally certified teachers, are test scores higher, and the answer is unambiguously yes."

Some subsequent studies find correlation between teachers' qualification and students' achievement (e.g., Croninger, Rice, Rathbun, & Nishio, 2007, as cited by Hasenfeld, 2010, p. 417). However, there are conflicting results from studies, with some showing no difference in outcomes for students taught by certified teachers compared to those taught by teachers without this certification (Rouse, 2008). According to Augsburg College education professor Vicki Olson,

> When you consider the impact of licensed vs. non-licensed teachers on student learning, the results are not all that different from the studies cited in the NRC report. Typically the licensed teachers get better results, but the studies vary and the differences are not huge. (personal communication, October 27, 2008)

In summary, we do not know enough yet from empirical research about what impact licensing has on actual helpfulness and quality of services in the lives of people who use them. However, as questions of regulatory effectiveness continue to emerge across the professions, rigorous studies are likely to follow. The framework for analysis of social work licensing presented in the next chapter will prompt students to find out what is known in their areas about the impact of licensing.

CHAPTER TWO

Contemporary Legal Landscape

THIS CHAPTER PRESENTS the basic principles that undergird regulation of social work practice (Agostinelli, 1973) and introduces readers to a framework for comparative analysis of regulatory legislation and policies. Informed by frameworks for international comparative analysis developed by policy scholars (e.g., Link & Bibus, 2000; Segal & Brzuzy, 1998; Tracy, 1992), this framework consists of a step-by-step series of questions for analyzing legal regulation of social work in their jurisdictions. The letters of the word "LICENSEE" help with organizing and remembering the steps of the analytical process:

Locate legal regulation of social work.

Identify the purpose of social work regulation and the formal definition of practice.

Cite the classification system and clarify coverage.

Explain any exemptions and elaborate.

Note what applicants need to do: the eligibility criteria they must meet and the application process they must follow.

Summarize standards of conduct or practice and the disciplinary or compliance process.

Examine strengths and weaknesses of current regulation; identify alternative strategies.

Evaluate actual and potential impacts of current regulation and proposed alternatives.

We will now elaborate these steps in more detail.

L

The first step directs readers to *locate* where to look for social work regulation in their jurisdiction's *legal landscape*—that is, which statutes, rules, government policies, and so on regulate social work practice. Are the regulations promulgated by the central national or federal government, by regional units (e.g., states or provinces), or under other legal auspices?

I

The second step is *identifying the purpose* of legal regulation as set forth in current law, rule, or policy (for example, to protect people who use social work services or to secure client safety). Among the questions to address in this step are how and by whom this purpose was established and what goals have been set to achieve this purpose. For example, how is the regulation system funded?

C

The third step is *citing* and *clarifying* where current law places the jurisdiction on the continuum of social work regulation or classifications from voluntary certification (least protection for clients) to licensing (most protection for clients). The official definition of social work practice is critical for this step; because of the complexity of social work practice, the definition's likely breadth, generality, and vagueness are often problematic (Payne, 2007a). What are the scopes of practice covered under social work regulation? Two other key questions to address during this step are, Who among social work practitioners comes under this regulation? and Are practitioners required to be credentialed, certified, registered, or licensed?

E

The fourth step involves identifying and *explaining any exemptions* allowed under the regulation. A common exemption is for students learning social work practice in agency settings under the supervision of social work field instructors as part of their practicum. Are any other groups exempted? Are all forms of social work practice covered, or only practice with individuals facing mental health difficulties (clinical treatment services)? Are there tiers or levels of sanctioned practice and regulatory rigor (e.g., associate, entry level, advanced)? Are there or were there grandparenting provisions that waived some requirements for a period when regulation was first established or expanded? Elaborating on the justification or rationale for each exemption and identifying who benefits are important tasks for fully understanding the limits of legal regulation.

N

The fifth step is *noting* and describing what social workers applying for approved status (e.g., their social work license) *need to do:* what educational qualifications and testing are required; what background checks applicants must submit to; what continuing education, preservice, or inservice training is expected; what share of the costs of regulation is borne by the applicant (usually through fees); whether and under what circumstances transfers from other jurisdictions are endorsed; what degree of supervision is required and for how long; and when renewals are scheduled.

S

The sixth step is *summarizing the standards* of conduct and practice established in regulation, the process for reporting when practitioners' decisions or actions fall below the thresholds set by those standards, the recourses available for securing safety and redressing harm, and disciplinary or corrective actions possible in cases of social workers' incompetent or unethical practice, misfeasance, malfeasance of duties, or other misconduct. What is the compliance process? How are privacy and due process rights ensured? Under what circumstances are the social worker's rights to practice removed or restricted? If they are removed or restricted, can they be restored? If so, how?

E_1

The seventh step is *examining* the strengths and weaknesses of the current system of regulation. How effective is it in achieving its purpose (second step above)? Who is affected? What have been its intended impacts? What have been its unintended effects, and are those effects positive or negative? Where are improvements needed, and what alternative legal strategies might work better than the current system?

E_2

The eighth and final step is *evaluating* the current system of regulation of social work practice and planning further evaluation of any proposed improvements. What actions do readers plan to take and how will their effectiveness be evaluated?

The rest of this chapter demonstrates how the LICENSEE framework can serve as a format for learning about social work regulations where students live or plan to work. Because most of us know little about the licensing process until we need to apply for a license, this step-by-step logical template for analysis is useful when beginning to study professional regulations and preparing to become a social worker. With detailed examples from Minnesota, where one of the authors (Bibus) lives and works, we present narrative findings at each step of the framework. (Table 3.2 in chapter 3 demonstrates how the framework could be used in a table format.)

We hope that the application of the LICENSEE framework to Minnesota's regulatory system will illustrate for students both potential content (such as definitions and other provisions directly from statutes or rules) and likely successful strategies for finding information needed to address each step in the template. We encourage students to seek data from a variety of sources beginning with local statutes and rules, local board websites, material, forms, documents and reports, and local board members and staff. ASWB's website and resources provide some local data as well as contact information for local jurisdictions; each state, territory, district, and province in Canada make substantive definitions and provisions available. The local chapter of NASW is another key resource, and licensed social workers (including field instructors and professors) and guest speakers in class can be most helpful. It is also possible that theses and other scholarly studies have analyzed local jurisdictions' regulatory policies, so conferring with reference librarians and conducting a literature search could be fruitful. National sources such as ASWB and Groshong's overview of clinical social work licensure (2009) provide comparisons of regulations from state to state. For example, Groshong presents comprehensive and readable tables using data from ASWB and other sources that show the variations of titles for licensed social workers, the types of boards governing social work practice, the kinds of exemptions in place, provisions related to continuing education, and other information related to clinical licensure. Using sixteen categories covering similar ground as the steps in LICENSEE, she also provides an analysis of regulations for clinical social work in Washington, DC, Delaware, and Virginia.

Locating Legal Landscape

The state of Minnesota has a practice act that sets standards and procedures for licensing social workers. It establishes the board of social work, which is then authorized to carry out the provisions of the statute. The state's governor appoints the fifteen members of the board for four-year terms; of those fifteen, five members especially represent the interests of the public and cannot be social workers themselves, while the rest are licensed social workers from various specified fields of practice. The board appoints an executive director, who in turn hires and supervises a complement of staff to carry out day-to-day operations of the board.

The board's website provides easy access to the relevant legislation, including two chapters in the state's legal code: Chapter 214 Examining and Licensing Boards, governing regulation generally, and Chapter 148D (148E effective August 1, 2011) Board of Social Work, governing regulation of social work practice (see http://www.socialwork.state.mn.us/).

Although the Social Work Board also has the power to make rules, in 2005 it decided to seek repeal of all its rules and incorporate them directly into statute, due to the difficulties inherent in the process of amending those rules (which was more strenuous and time-consuming than seeking amendments to the legislation itself). Currently, it has promulgated no rules in addition to the legislative statute. Administrative procedures are set forth and forms are available on the board's website.

Identifying the Purpose

Minnesota's Board of Social Work's practice act does not explicitly state an overall purpose. This curious omission is a historical artifact of the legislature's reluctance to encode broad purpose statements in any area of legislation for fear of inviting lawsuits against which it would be difficult to defend. Thus, to find the purpose, one must first look at the duties assigned to the board (see box 2.1). At the instigation of professional social workers (e.g., the Minnesota chapter of the NASW), in 1987 the legislature passed on a close vote and the governor signed the first legislation establishing the Board of Social Work and its duties. (For a detailed history, see Bibus, 2007.) In a passage deeper into the current practice act, there is a statement of the purpose of the compliance provisions of the statute, which drafters in 2005 were able to get passed by the legislature. These provisions deal with enforcement of the professional standards and licensing process, the procedures for clients and others to submit complaints about a particular licensee, and discipline of licensees whose practice falls below standards. Funding of the board to carry out its duties and purpose is entirely reliant on fees such as those paid by applicants, licensees, and, to a lesser extent, continuing education providers.

Citing and Clarifying Classifications

The official definition of social work practice is set in the board's practice act, Minnesota Statute (MS) 148D.010 (see box 2.2). As is clear from the definition, social work practice in Minnesota covers a wide range of

Box 2.1 Minnesota Statutes, Board of Social Work Practice Act

148D.015 SCOPE.

This chapter applies to all applicants and licensees, all persons who use the title social worker, and all persons in or out of this state who provide social work services to clients who reside in this state unless there are specific applicable exemptions provided by law.

148D.030 DUTIES OF THE BOARD.

Subdivision 1. Duties.
The board must perform the duties necessary to promote and protect the public health, safety, and welfare through the licensure and regulation of persons who practice social work in this state. These duties include, but are not limited to:

(1) establishing the qualifications and procedures for individuals to be licensed as social workers;
(2) establishing standards of practice for social workers;
(3) holding examinations or contracting with the Association of Social Work Boards or a similar examination body designated by the board to hold examinations to assess applicants' qualifications;
(4) issuing licenses to qualified individuals pursuant to sections 148D.055 and 148D.060;
(5) taking disciplinary, adversarial, corrective, or other action pursuant to sections 148D.255 to 148D.270 when an individual violates the requirements of this chapter;
(6) assessing fees pursuant to sections 148D.175 and 148D.180; and
(7) educating social workers and the public on the requirements of the board.

148D.185 PURPOSE OF COMPLIANCE LAWS.

The purpose of sections 148D.185 to 148D.290 is to protect the public by ensuring that all persons licensed as social workers meet minimum standards of practice. The board shall promptly and fairly investigate and resolve all complaints alleging violations of statutes and rules that the board is empowered to enforce and (1) take appropriate disciplinary action, adversarial action, or other action justified by the facts, or (2) enter into corrective action agreements or stipulations to cease practice, when doing so is consistent with the board's obligation to protect the public.

BOX 2.2: DEFINITION OF SOCIAL WORK PRACTICE IN MINNESOTA STATUTE 148.D

Subd. 9. Practice of social work.

(a) "Practice of social work" means working to maintain, restore, or improve behavioral, cognitive, emotional, mental, or social functioning of clients, in a manner that applies accepted professional social work knowledge, skills, and values, including the person-in-environment perspective, by providing in person or through telephone, video conferencing, or electronic means one or more of the social work services described in paragraph (b), clauses (1) to (3). Social work services may address conditions that impair or limit behavioral, cognitive, emotional, mental, or social functioning. Such conditions include, but are not limited to, the following: abuse and neglect of children or vulnerable adults, addictions, developmental disorders, disabilities, discrimination, illness, injuries, poverty, and trauma. Practice of social work also means providing social work services in a position for which the educational basis is the individual's degree in social work described in subdivision 13.

(b) Social work services include:

  (1) providing assessment and intervention through direct contact with clients, developing a plan based on information from an assessment, and providing services which include, but are not limited to, assessment, case management, client-centered advocacy, client education, consultation, counseling, crisis intervention, and referral;

  (2) providing for the direct or indirect benefit of clients through administrative, educational, policy, or research services including, but not limited to:

   (i) advocating for policies, programs, or services to improve the well-being of clients;

   (ii) conducting research related to social work services;

   (iii) developing and administering programs which provide social work services;

   (iv) engaging in community organization to address social problems through planned collective action;

   (v) supervising individuals who provide social work services to clients;

   (vi) supervising social workers in order to comply with the supervised practice requirements specified in sections 148D.100 to 148D.125; and

   (vii) teaching professional social work knowledge, skills, and values to students; and

  (3) engaging in clinical practice.

Box 2.2: (CONTINUED)

Subd. 6. Clinical practice.

"Clinical practice" means applying professional social work knowledge, skills, and values in the differential diagnosis and treatment of psychosocial function, disability, or impairment, including addictions and emotional, mental, and behavioral disorders. Treatment includes a plan based on a differential diagnosis. Treatment may include, but is not limited to, the provision of psychotherapy to individuals, couples, families, and groups. Clinical social workers may also provide the services described in subdivision 9.

---

practice arenas, from direct service with individuals to policy practice, community organization, advocacy, supervision, and teaching. The practice act delineates that any person practicing social work as defined in the law must have a current Minnesota license to practice social work unless there is an explicit exemption in statute. In 2009, the definition was clarified to specify, "practice of social work also means providing social work services in a position for which the educational basis is the individual's degree in social work." As discussed below, in addition to the usual exemption for students learning to practice social work in practicum settings under supervision of field instructors from accredited social work programs, there is a significant and controversial exemption for social workers employed by city, county, or state social service agencies (e.g., child protective services social workers). Minnesota has four social work licenses (see box 2.3 for descriptions of each license):

- Licensed Social Worker (LSW),
- Licensed Graduate Social Worker (LGSW),
- Licensed Independent Social Worker (LISW), and
- Licensed Independent Clinical Social Worker (LICSW).

Explaining Exemptions

With a fairly comprehensive and inclusive definition of social work practice, the practice act in Minnesota covers the scope of practice set forth in the ASWB's model act. For example, there is a license for social workers who have a BSW degree but who do not have an MSW degree, and there is another license for those who have an MSW degree. However, in addition to the usual exemption for students learning social work practice in

Box 2.3 Four Social Work Licenses in Minnesota

148D.050 LICENSING; SCOPE OF PRACTICE.

Subdivision 1. Requirements.
A person licensed under section 148D.055 or 148D.061 must comply with the requirements of subdivision 2, 3, 4, or 5.

Subd. 2. Licensed social worker.
A licensed social worker may engage in social work practice except that a licensed social worker must not engage in clinical practice.

Subd. 3. Licensed graduate social worker.
A licensed graduate social worker may engage in social work practice except that a licensed graduate social worker must not engage in clinical practice except under the supervision of a licensed independent clinical social worker or an alternate supervisor pursuant to section 148D.120.

Subd. 4. Licensed independent social worker.
A licensed independent social worker may engage in social work prac-tice except that a licensed independent social worker must not engage in clinical practice except under the supervision of a licensed independent clinical social worker or an alternate supervisor pursuant to section 148D.120.

Subd. 5. Licensed independent clinical social worker.
A licensed independent clinical social worker may engage in social work practice, including clinical practice.

agency settings under the supervision of social work field instructors as part of their practicum, there are significant other exemptions in Minneso-ta's practice act (see box 2.4). The exemption that affects the most people (practitioners as well as clients) makes licensing voluntary for social work-ers employed by county social service agencies. Over the years since this exemption was first established as part of the original practice act in Min-nesota in 1987, the Minnesota Board of Social Work has recognized that this exemption inhibits its statutory purpose of promoting and protecting the public health, safety, and welfare through the licensure and regulation of persons who practice social work in Minnesota (MS 148D.030 Subd. 1. Duties). At its July 27, 2001, meeting, the board approved by unanimous vote the recommendation from its Special Committee on Board Operations to "seek legislation repealing all licensure exemptions, so that all social workers practicing in Minnesota are required to be licensed." This was

BOX 2.4 EXEMPTIONS

148D.065 EXEMPTIONS.

Subdivision 1. Other professionals.
Nothing in this chapter may be construed to prevent members of other professions or occupations from performing functions for which they are qualified or licensed. This exception includes but is not limited to: licensed physicians, registered nurses, licensed practical nurses, licensed psychologists, psychological practitioners, probation officers, members of the clergy and Christian Science practitioners, attorneys, marriage and family therapists, alcohol and drug counselors, professional counselors, school counselors, and registered occupational therapists or certified occupational therapist assistants. These persons must not, however, hold themselves out to the public by any title or description stating or implying that they are engaged in the practice of social work, or that they are licensed to engage in the practice of social work. Persons engaged in the practice of social work are not exempt from the board's jurisdiction solely by the use of one of the titles in this subdivision.

Subd. 2. Students.
An internship, externship, or any other social work experience that is required for the completion of an accredited program of social work does not constitute the practice of social work under this chapter.

Subd. 3. Geographic waiver.
A geographic waiver may be granted by the board on a case-by-case basis to agencies with special regional hiring problems. The waiver is for the purpose of permitting agencies to hire individuals who do not meet the qualifications of section 148D.055 or 148D.060 to practice social work.

Subd. 4. City, county, and state agency social workers.
The licensure of city, county, and state agency social workers is voluntary. City, county, and state agencies employing social workers are not required to employ licensed social workers.

Subd. 5. Tribes and private nonprofit agencies; voluntary licensure.
The licensure of social workers who are employed by federally recognized tribes, or by private nonprofit agencies whose primary service focus addresses ethnic minority populations, and who are themselves members of ethnic minority populations within those agencies, is voluntary.

understood to be a lengthy process extending perhaps more than ten years. A task force has recently mobilized the political support to introduce legislation modifying this exemption.

According to Alan Ingram, executive director of the local chapter of NASW, and other key informants, the original arguments in favor of the exemption for county workers were that

1. licensing was not needed in the counties for public protection because the elected commissioners who govern the counties were public officials who provided oversight and accountability,
2. there was a satisfactory process already in place for handling complaints or grievances by clients, and
3. the layers of supervision within county social services ensured competency and standards.

A leader in the coalition of social workers who were advocating for licensing stated that their strategy was to get a foot in the door with licensing legislation and then go back to the legislature and have the exemptions repealed soon thereafter. As noted above, twenty years later the Minnesota Board of Social Work is still working on the goal of modifying the exemption for city, county, and state social workers; if it is successful, there will likely be a period of grandparenting similar to that in effect for a short time at initial licensure in 1987 and when an exemption for social workers in hospitals and nursing homes was repealed in 1995. (About 38% of the approximately 3,400 county social workers in Minnesota maintain their social work license voluntarily; there are about 10,500 licensed social workers in the state.) The other categories for exemption, such as the geographic waiver and the voluntary licensing of social workers employed by American Indian tribes, affect far fewer practitioners and clients, though they do raise concerns regarding protection and recourse offered to clients of social workers who choose not to be licensed.

Noting What Applicants Need to Do

The steps that candidates for social work licensure need to follow are clearly laid out in Minnesota state law. First, applicants for a social work license must provide the board with evidence (such as an official transcript) that they have a BSW or MSW degree in social work from an undergraduate or graduate program accredited by the U.S. Council on Social Work Education (CSWE), the Canadian Association of Schools of Social

Work, or a similar accrediting body designated by the Minnesota Board of Social Work.

Second, applicants must pass the ASWB examination for the license to which they are applying (e.g., the bachelor's examination for applicants to the Licensed Social Worker [LSW]); the applicant may take the examination before completing the social work degree program. The examination may not be taken more than three times without passing, although the board is authorized to approve any subsequent attempt under certain circumstances (such as when the applicant's efforts are likely to improve his or her score and there are letters of recommendation from two licensed social workers).

In rare situations involving applicants who are from other countries and for whom English is a second learned language, an alternative path to licensure in Minnesota is available if the applicant does not obtain a passing score on the ASWB examination. This provisional license was adopted to respond to an unexplained trend whereby some otherwise apparently competent applicants were not passing the examination despite repeated efforts, and there was a shortage of licensees ready to serve immigrant groups (although provisional licensees are not required to restrict their practice to any particular population). Provisional licensees must submit to rigorous supervision requirements as a method of demonstrating competency in lieu of the examination. Fewer than 2 percent of social work licensees in Minnesota have been licensed under this provisional process and its predecessor alternative path for candidates who are both born outside the United States and for whom English is a second learned language.

Third, the application form must be complete and signed; it requires identifying information, name(s), home and mailing addresses, telephone numbers, e-mail address, social security number, educational information, identifying and contact information on the applicant's current employer(s), and so on; date of birth, gender, and ethnic background are optional. A criminal background check must be completed, and applicants must truthfully and completely answer eleven "Standards of Practice Questions." These questions include the following:

- whether the applicant has pled guilty to or been convicted of misdemeanors or felonies, including traffic offenses involving the use of alcohol or drugs;
- whether the applicant has ever been disciplined, sanctioned, or found to have violated a professional association's code of ethics or any licensing code;

- whether the applicant has ever been terminated from or been subjected to disciplinary action in any position;
- whether the applicant has ever practiced social work without a license or falsely used the title "social worker" or assisted another to do so;
- whether the applicant has ever been disciplined, forced to withdraw, or been investigated by a postsecondary educational institution because of alleged misconduct of any kind; and
- whether illness, use of alcohol or drugs, or other conditions impair the applicant's capacity to practice.

To be eligible for licensure, applicants must not have engaged in conduct that would be a violation of practice standards established in the practice act.

Finally, fees such as those for application, examinations, and the license itself must be paid; depending on the license and examination, those fees total between $300 and $400. By completing and signing the application, applicants give legal authority to the Board of Social Work as the law states: "to investigate any information provided or requested in the application. The board may request that the applicant provide additional information, verification, or documentation." Practice of social work without a license is not allowed except in exempt settings specified in the law.

Applicants who have a social work license from another jurisdiction (state, province, and so on) must provide information concerning their current license; if the requirements for that license meet Minnesota's requirements (such as passing the ASWB examination, background checks, and so on), the applicant may be eligible for what is called "endorsement" and licensure in Minnesota. There is no official reciprocity whereby Minnesota recognizes any social work license from a given state or other jurisdiction as equivalent. There are provisions for licensees from other states to obtain a temporary license under certain circumstances; in some situations (such as for social work faculty from other countries who have moved to Minnesota to teach for a year), a temporary, time-limited license is also available.

Once the license is granted, the licensee must renew it every two years. In the renewal application (which can be completed online), all information gathered during the initial application is updated, the licensee answers the Standards of Practice Questions again, and documents that the required number of hours of continuing education have been completed; in 2011 for most licensees forty hours will be required over the two-year renewal period, two of which must be on ethics. If the licensee is still fulfilling the supervisory requirements of his or her license, a supervision plan must be submitted when licensed practice begins. In addition, the licensee must submit the supervisor's identifying information (including credentials and license status) plus verification and a report by the supervisor of the supervision hours completed and content covered with a signed recommendation regarding the licensee's practice. The licensee also submits the requisite fee for two more years of the license to practice social work in Minnesota. Beginning in 2011, applicants for the clinical license have additional requirements for clinical supervision and for educational preparation and continuing education within specified clinical content areas.

Fees collected from applicants and licensees constitute the funding mechanism for the regulation of social work in Minnesota. The state provides no support to the Board of Social Work from the general fund generated by taxes. Indeed, in recent years—because the state has faced budget deficits—it has taken money from the board's accumulated budget reserves (i.e., licensees' fees) to offset part of the state's budget shortfall in other areas.

Summarizing Standards

Minnesota's practice act is composed of two major parts. The first, whose provisions are summarized above, regulates the process of licensure. The second establishes standards to which licensees are to be held accountable, and the process for investigating and responding to situations when licensees' practice is alleged to have fallen below standards. This latter part of the practice act begins with a purpose statement clarifying that licensing of social workers in Minnesota is carried out in order "to protect the public by ensuring that all persons licensed as social workers meet minimum standards of practice" (MS 148D.185). It then sets forth grounds for action on the part of the Minnesota Board of Social Work when a social worker violates the statutes enforced by the board; a federal or state law related to the practice of social work; or an order, stipulation, or agreement issued by the board. A licensee's conduct before being licensed is also covered, if that conduct did not meet with "minimum accepted and prevailing standards of professional social work practice" or "adversely affects the applicant's or licensee's ability to practice" in accordance with the standards set in statute. Unauthorized practice is also defined as practicing outside the scope of one's license or competencies or without a license (unless in an exempt setting). Requirements for proper "conspicuous" display of one's license and information for clients on how to contact the Board of Social Work as well as prohibitions on representing oneself falsely are detailed. For example, persons in Minnesota cannot legally present themselves using the title "social worker" unless they are licensed as such or practice in an exempt setting.

Next in the statute are provisions requiring social workers to practice only within areas of competence; they are not to hold themselves out as competent beyond the extent of their education, training, license, and so on, but instead are to make appropriate referral for clients to other practitioners who are competent if clients need services beyond the licensee's competence. Even when licensees have completed the hours of supervision required for their license, they must still obtain supervision or consultation whenever "appropriate or necessary for competent or ethical practice." Proper delegation of responsibilities is covered. Grounds for taking action if a social worker is unable to practice competently and safely because of impairments due to illness, use of alcohol or drugs, or other impairing condition are set in statute.

A lengthy and detailed set of standards of professional and ethical conduct follow (MS 148D.205–240). These regulations cover conduct or failure to act that is unethical whether or not it causes harm to clients, interns, students, supervisees, or the public. Conduct that has the potential to harm or demonstrates "willful or careless disregard for the health, welfare, or safety of a client, intern, student, or supervisee" is cause for the board to act. Responsibilities to clients are enumerated, including respecting clients' best interest in self-determination (unless another law requires the licensee to do otherwise, such as when the licensee must report that a client has abused her or his child). Licensees must not discriminate against others "on the basis of age, gender, sexual orientation, race, color, national origin, religion, illness, disability, political affiliation, or social or economic status." Licensees must follow accepted protocols for protection of human subjects during research. Licensees have the legal responsibility to maintain professional boundaries with current and former clients, students, interns, or supervisees; to refrain from engaging in or suggesting any sexual relationships with current clients, students, interns, or supervisees; and to not engage in personal, sexual, or business relationships that exploit, deceive, manipulate, or coerce current or former clients. These provisions also apply to relationships with clients' family or household members. Licensees cannot legally give alcohol or drugs to clients unless explicitly permitted to do so by law (such as in legally sanctioned distribution of prescribed medication), nor can they legally accept alcoholic beverages from clients.

The next section of the statute details standards regarding treatment and intervention services (MS 148D.225) including assessment or diagnosis, service planning, record keeping, and termination of services or referral. In the section that follows this, confidentiality in practice and records is covered with provisions on informed consent, data privacy, and release of information regarding clients. There are specific regulations governing the release of information only with clients' consent in most cases or without consent in certain circumstances, such as when the social worker has a duty to warn others who may be in harm's way due to threatened action on the part of a client. State regulations surrounding licensees' practices regarding setting fees and billing for their services also are provided. Finally, licensees must report to the board within ninety days if they have violated licensing rules or laws or committed crimes related to the practice of social work or any other crime; in addition to being mandatory reporters of child and adult maltreatment, licensees also are required to report conduct by other licensees of all the health-related disciplines when that conduct violates the standards set in statute or rules of the relevant board and to report unlicensed practice by others.

In the next section of the practice act the authority and procedures of the Board of Social Work are established to enforce the standards above and respond to complaints that a social worker's practice has fallen below minimum standards (MS 148D.245). Investigative powers and procedures (such as subpoenas, ordering mental or physical examinations or chemical dependency evaluations, and notifications to complainants and licensees subject to complaints) are detailed. An attempt has been made to limit the board's investigative powers to focus reasonably only on conduct related to the practice of social work. Even in cases that under most circumstances would be immediately investigated, if the investigation involves a case of a vulnerable child or adult that is already before the courts, the board may suspend its investigation upon request until the court issues findings.

Licensees are obliged to cooperate with the board's investigation. If the board's investigation results in substantiation of the complaint that the licensee's practice fell below standards or violated the licensing statute in some other way, this part of the law provides for the range of actions that the board can consider. It can take disciplinary action such as revoking or suspending a license or placing conditions on the licensee's practice. Fines or additional fees or reimbursement for costs of the investigation are permitted. Reprimands are also possible. Licensees may request a formal hearing before the board to contest these actions; licensees may also stipulate agreement with the findings and disciplinary measures. A number of actions that the law calls "adversarial but nondisciplinary" (MS 148D.265) include automatic suspensions of a license if the licensee is committed as mentally incompetent, orders to cease and desist practice, and restraining orders if continuing practice would bring imminent risk of harm to others.

These disciplinary and adversarial actions are rarely taken. For example, there are usually between one hundred and two hundred complaints received per year, or ten to twenty complaints for every 1,000 licensees; the most frequent category of complaints by far involves practice issues such as failure to properly implement a service plan (Minnesota Board of Social Work, 2008). Instead, most investigations of complaints are not substantiated or the board has no jurisdiction; or, if substantiated, the licensee and board agree on the corrective action to be taken. These agreements are quite formal, written, detailed, and legally binding. Similar to the disciplinary and adversarial actions, they are public and employers or others can have access to the agreements and their status. There are conditions and deadlines set for successful completion of the agreement with the burden of proof of success placed on the licensee. If the agreement is fulfilled, the licensee can resume practice as usual (though the agreement stays on the licensee's record).

Minnesota's practice act ends with sections forbidding unlicensed practice of social work and governing the use of the title "social worker," and then sets forth conditions under which employers and professional associations must report to the Board of Social Work when an employee or member who is licensed as a social worker has been subject to discipline or other sanction or adversarial action for conduct that violates the standards in the practice act. These mandatory reporters have immunity from civil liability or criminal prosecution, assuming they have reported in good faith. The final provision of the act establishes violations (such as failure to report) as misdemeanors. As described below, however, there is a process for reporters to make their complaint to a diversionary program instead of to the Board of Social Work when the licensee or applicant is impaired.

In Minnesota, the law covering licensing of all of the health-related professions provides for an alternative to board discipline. In cases when an illness or other condition (such as addiction to alcohol or drugs) appears to be impairing a licensee's practice, a diversionary program called the Health Professionals Service Program (HPSP) can become involved. Self-reporting is also possible. Upon agreement with the licensee, HPSP monitors the licensee's compliance with a treatment plan intended to address the impairment so that the licensee's practice is safe and competent. If this intervention is successful, the relevant board does not assume jurisdiction regarding the complaint involved and takes no disciplinary action. If the licensee does not cooperate with HPSP, the board becomes involved to investigate and address the original complaint with all the disciplinary and corrective powers described above.

Examining Strengths and Weaknesses

In its strategic planning process and in recent reports to the legislature, the Board of Social work has published what it has found to be successful in carrying out its mission of public protection by setting and enforcing minimum standards of social work practice since social work licensing began in Minnesota in 1987. It also has identified major threats to its ability to carry out its mission. Those threats include political realities (such as any exemptions or the absence of any state funding), internal accountability (such as a definition of social work practice that can withstand legal questions in contested hearings and other compliance judgments), opposition from other groups (such as unions), and lack of public understanding of the role of the board and misconceptions regarding its duties (summarized from the board's strategic plan, July 2007, available at http://www .socialwork.state.mn.us). Strategies are being developed to address these threats, and there have been a series of research studies identifying some of the intended and unintended effects of social work licensing in Minnesota.

Generally, according to evaluations and reports thus far, the purpose of licensing social workers in Minnesota has been achieved: people in the state using the services of licensed social workers can know the level of minimum competence of their social worker, and they have recourse to a regulatory board with legal powers to address lapses in practice. However, this public protection is not universal. For example, while the establishment of licensing for social workers in Minnesota twenty years ago has apparently led to a more consistently competent workforce of social workers in nonexempt settings, the exemption for county social workers also has led to confusion and inconsistencies in understanding who is a social worker and what is social work practice; thus, the protection of people using social work services is weaker than intended. In addition, the Board of Social Work can regulate only individual practitioners and has no authority over agencies, organizations, or employers.

There also have been concerns that requiring social workers to be licensed may have the unintended effect of reducing the access of some people to social work services. A recent report to the legislature pointed out that there are indeed shortages of licensed social workers who are persons of color or who are located in rural areas. People with physical or cognitive impairments, mental illness, who are older, living in poverty or homeless do not have as adequate access to licensed social workers as needed (Black-Hughes, 2008). In response to this and other studies (e.g., Alexander & Johnston, 2008; Bibus, 2007), the board has recommended to the legislature a multifaceted response including more and better data collection, addressing unnecessary barriers to licensing, increasing the representation of ethnically, racially, and culturally diverse groups in the regulation of social work practice, modifying the exemption for county social workers, increasing public education outreach, collaborating with stakeholder groups, and providing more incentives for practitioners to become licensed social workers (such as student loan forgiveness).

Evaluating the Licensing System in Minnesota

As noted above, the Minnesota Board of Social Work has undergone a recent process of strategic planning and also has completed a comprehensive series of reports to the legislature (see http://www.socialwork.state .mn.us). As a result, there is a current agenda in place for issues to address and improvements to seek in the system of regulation of social work practice in Minnesota. The most critical in terms of the board's mission to protect the public is modifying (i.e., limiting) the exemption for social workers employed in public agency settings. Thus, coauthor Bibus has devoted service and research time and attention to committee work and reports to prepare for introducing legislative amendments to state statute to modify the exemption for county social workers. Other agenda items emerging from the board's strategic plan also will be worthy of tracking and working in partnership with the local chapter of NASW and others, including expanded training and educational offerings in supervision, avoiding increases in fees, increasing the diversity of and access to licensed social workers and licensing supervisors, and tightening the compliance process by decreasing processing time and providing more information and better records when possible.

As the description of Minnesota's regulations above demonstrates, using a narrative approach to address the steps in the LICENSEE framework fosters in-depth and comprehensive analysis. An alternative approach, using a table in spreadsheet format, provides snapshots of each step that serve well for comparisons across jurisdictions. In the following chapter, both the narrative and table approaches are used as templates to explore variations in social work regulation in a sample of countries around the world.

CHAPTER THREE

The Regulation of
Social Work Worldwide

With Contributions by Monit Cheung, Subhabrata Dutta,
Chathapuram Ramanathan, and Malcolm Payne

In conclusion, we believe that the scope of international social work open
to social work graduates is expanding rapidly, and that more and more
social workers are being drawn into the international field, either as a
career or for short periods that inform and complement their international
approach to their work at the national and local level. (Cox & Pawar, 2006,
p. 371)

WHILE THE MAIN FOCUS OF THIS PRIMER is social work licensing in the
United States, today's helping professionals, especially social workers, practice with a global perspective. It is no longer possible (if it ever was) for
social workers to have an exclusively domestic or parochial focus. As Link
and Healy (2005) write, "There is no room for ignorance of the rest of
the world because we are all so closely intertwined" (p. vi). Therefore, in
accordance with educational policies established by the CSWE; 2008, EP
2.1.1, 2.1.2, 2.1.5, & 2.1.9, today's social work students in America learn to
identify as professional social workers who are guided by global awareness
and understanding and are ready to respond to contexts that shape practice, including "the global interconnections of oppression," international
codes of ethics and other relevant laws, human rights, and globalization
itself.

Beyond gaining awareness and understanding of transnational dynamics such as the process of globalization, students may have an interest
in exploring opportunities to practice social work in other lands. Before
embarking on such a global professional journey, students should first
investigate the regulatory environment in nations they are considering for
career possibilities. The LICENSEE framework of analysis from chapter 2
could prove useful in preparation for this exploration. (See references cited

here such as Cox & Pawar 2006, as well appendix B for more information on prospective opportunities for field practicum placements in other countries and the issues related to professional mobility across borders.) This chapter begins, then, with a brief overview of the status of social work around the world. Next, applying the LICENSEE framework, three guest contributors provide detailed descriptions of the current structure of regulation of social work practice in Asia, India, and the United Kingdom.

Overview

Globalization

Integrating the analyses of scholars of international social work and social welfare development, Tan and Rowlands (2004) come to a broad and evolving definition of globalization "as a complex multifaceted process involving the internationalization of the market economy, the rapid growth and expansion of communications technologies, the creation of new forms of media, innovative modes of governance, judicial norms and power relations" (pp. 16–17; see also the various definitions of globalization in the appendix to International Federation of Social Workers' [IFSW, 2005] policy statement on globalization and the environment). Recent globalization has had profound, pervasive, and sometimes unrecognized effects on social workers' relationships with clients. However, Healy and Hokenstad (2008) point to indigenization as a countervailing dynamic that is especially pertinent to social work regulation; this term refers to appropriately focusing helping efforts locally with ethical sensitivity to indigenous cultural, ethnic, religious, political, and economic forces as well as local norms and needs. (See Healy, 2001, pp. 35–38; Elliott and Mayadas, 1999, p. 54; and Abo-El-Nasr, 1997, and Mayadas et al., 1997, e.g., pp. 216–217, 443–447.) Practice and regulation of practice will always and necessarily take place in situ—that is, locally; we work in our immediate physical, social, political, and geographical locale and regulatory jurisdiction. Nevertheless, social work's perspective on people in their environments must also simultaneously take into account global conditions. (Hence, Lyons and colleagues 2006 chose the following compound phrase for the subtitle of their text on international social work: global conditions and local practice.)

Tan and Rowlands (2004) conclude, "undeniably, the forces of globalization are changing the context for social work practice" (p. 124). Similarly, after examining the evolving definitions of and perspectives toward the phenomenon of globalization, Lyons and colleagues (2006) suggest that one of its important characteristics is "a gradual recognition (perhaps not yet fully achieved) that patterns of behavior in one country or part of the world can have profound implications for whole populations in other societies or perhaps even worldwide" (p. 23). For example, in many parts of the United States, social workers routinely have contact with clients and other professionals who have international as well as multicultural backgrounds; thus, social workers must be able not only to recognize challenges such as language and other cultural differences, but also to tap the strengths that come with such fresh experiences and the adept navigation needed for living in new lands. As Payne (2007a) observes, "If the social origins of the issues that face people in their lives are global, then the claim to have an impact through interpersonal work requires that social work must find ways of achieving and understanding global challenges" (p. 179).

Fortunately, social work is becoming a global profession. (See Healy, 2001, for a succinct historical summary of the international dimensions of social work over the past century.) The International Federation of Social Worker's (IFSW's) International Statement on Globalization and the Environment (IFSW, 2005) puts social work four square in position to amplify the benefits of globalization and to buffer its damaging effects:

> Globalisation is the process by which all peoples and communities come to experience an increasingly common economic, social and cultural environment. By definition, the process affects everybody throughout the world.
>
> A more integrated world community brings both benefits and problems for all; it affects the balance of economic, political and cultural power between nations, communities and individuals and it can both enhance and limit freedoms and human rights. Social workers, by the nature of their work, tend to meet those who are more likely to have suffered the damaging consequences of some aspects of globalisation.
>
> Social workers approach globalisation from a human rights perspective as set out in the IFSW [International Federation of Social Workers] international Ethical Documents for social work. Social workers recognise the benefits and disadvantages of globalisation for the most vulnerable people in the world. Our professional perspective focuses especially on how the economic and environmental consequences affect social relationships and individual opportunity. (http://www.ifsw.org/p38000222.html)

Status of Social Work Professional Regulation Globally

Social workers are likely practicing today in nearly every country. However, public recognition of the profession as manifested by the presence of a program of social work education, a professional association of social workers, or legal regulation of social work practice varies greatly. According to Cox and Pawar (2006, p. 20), "The current reality is that social work is virtually nonexistent in all of the poorest countries of the world," which represent about 25 percent of the world's nations (see http://www.un.org/special-rep/ohrlls/ldc/list.htm). The extent to which social work practice is regulated in the remaining approximately 145 nation-states ranges widely from full-fledged licensing or registration throughout the United States and Canada to expanding and developing regulation in the United Kingdom and Asian nations (for example). Other countries rely on social work education programs to set standards of entry into the profession and have had no more than preliminary discussions on regulating practice postgraduation (e.g., Mexico, as we will see later in this chapter). After reviewing reports on social work globally, Cox and Pawar (2006) state,

> It is clear that organized professional social work exists to varying degrees in the majority of countries (many Least Developed Countries being the exception), and that the various national social work structures recognize each other as sharing much in common and as being part of a global profession. (p. 7)

The number of countries whose national professional association of social workers are members of the IFSW is ninety as of this writing, representing a total of about 745,000 social workers worldwide. Among the purposes of IFSW is promotion of social work as a profession through international cooperation in gaining recognition of social work and setting standards of practice (see www.ifsw.org). More than 400 schools of social work are listed as members of another major global social work association: the International Association of Schools of Social Work (IASSW). The first International Conference of Social Work in 1928 resulted in an early definition of social work (Healy, 2001, p. 80). At the turn of the twenty-first century, the IFSW and IASSW joined efforts in revising an international definition of social work and a general statement of principles for international ethics in social work (IFSW & IASSW, 2004). In the lengthy and systematic process used to develop this new definition and code (begun in 1996; Healy, 2001, p. 98), licensure laws and regulations were reviewed, and the process of updating and revising the definition and codes will no doubt continue (Hare, 2004).

Subsequently, the IFSW and IASSW worked to establish a set of Global Standards for the Education and Training of the Social Work Profession (IFSW & IASSW, 2004). This landmark document functions as a guide and an ideal toward which social work educators, students, practitioners, and regulators in every country can aspire. For example, standards with regard to values and ethical codes of conduct of the social work profession include Standard 9.3 setting the goal of "registration of professional staff and social work student . . . with national and/or regional regulatory (whether statutory or non-statutory) bodies, with defined codes of ethics"; and Standard 9.6 "ensuring that regulatory social work bodies are broadly representative of the social work profession, including [social workers and] . . . the direct participation of service users."

In introducing her survey of the members of the IASSW to see to what degree member schools were meeting the global standards, Barretta-Herman (2008) summarizes the debate concerning the need for or relevance of a global standard of social work practice. Some authors have questioned the very concept of global standards for as disparate a collection of "social works" as constitutes the social work profession. (Some even refer to the social work professions in plural; see Lyons and colleagues 2006, for example.) Even though social workers share a common set of values, social work practice standards must be driven fundamentally by local culture, values, norms, and demands. Others cite the wide disparities in resources such as educational opportunities and basic supports between different parts of the world. There also are tensions inherent in trying to join competing values such as the primacy that dominant Western culture gives to self-reliance, individual rights, and freedoms in contrast to the appreciation for the role of mutual responsibility, collective nurturing, and communal power cherished in many indigenous cultures and those of the global East and South. Conversely, while social work practice and professional identity are rooted in local values, they also are affected by global dynamics. "[Lyons] sees the Global Standards as the recognition of the transnational mobility of social workers and as an acknowledgment of the impact of global events on local practice" (Barretta-Herman, 2008, p. 824).

Comparing the approaches countries take to regulating such a dynamic and diverse profession can thus be instructive both in their common elements and in their unique qualities. Hence, we asked three colleagues who have expertise in how other countries regulate social work practice to apply the LICENSEE framework in describing social work regulation in the United Kingdom (Payne), in selected Asian nations (Cheung), and in India (Dutta & Ramanathan). We also provide a brief description of regulation of social work practice in the two countries that border the United States. (See Weiss & Welbourne, 2007, for recent summaries of the status of the profession and regulation in India, Mexico, the United Kingdom, and the United States.)

Social Work Regulations in the United Kingdom
Malcolm Payne, BA, DipSS, PhD

The United Kingdom of Great Britain and Northern Ireland (UK) is an archipelago of islands off the northwestern coast of Europe, with a population of more than 60 million. It is the source of the English language; in addition to language, many aspects of its culture have similarities with American and Canadian culture. Therefore, many social workers and other professionals from North America thinking of practicing abroad consider the UK as an option. UK and North American social work education and agency organization have an interconnected history, with the result that transferring knowledge and skills appears to be easier than it does with some other countries. Moreover, there is a national shortage of social workers in the UK and North American social work courses have a high reputation, so agencies may well be interested in employing North American practitioners; immigration legislation, which generally limits employment of non–European Union citizens, may open the way for North American applicants because of the shortage.

Looking at the UK also provides an interesting comparator with the licensing system in American states and Canadian provinces and in other countries, although UK social workers are registered rather than licensed. This section starts with a brief introduction to the organization of social services and social policy in the UK, so that a non-UK reader can make sense of the context of social work regulation in the UK. It then examines the UK system following the LICENSEE template used in this book.

UK Social Service Organization and Social Policy

The UK comprises four main countries: England (by far the largest in terms of population and other dimensions), Northern Ireland, Scotland, and Wales; some smaller islands are not technically part of these countries and have separate legal and administrative systems (Payne & Shardlow, 2002). The term "Great Britain" applies only to England, Scotland, and Wales, and excludes Northern Ireland; this was a legal entity before the UK was established. The Republic of Ireland occupies the larger part of the second largest island in the group and is a separate country, with distinct systems. Each UK nation has separate legislation, a different system for organizing social services, and separate regulation of social work. However, the regulators work together so that the licensing arrangements are broadly similar, although requirements vary because, for example, social workers in Scotland will have legal knowledge to acquire that is different from the legal knowledge needed by a social worker in England.

Social services are referred to in the UK by the umbrella term "social care." Most services are provided within local government and most social workers are employed by local government councils in each locality. In England and Wales, social work is divided between children's social care, usually placed in a children and family division of the council's education department, and adult social care, usually a stand-alone department of the council but sometimes part of larger units, including, for example, housing. In Northern Ireland, social workers are part of specialized health and social services boards. In Scotland, social work includes services for adult offenders, and is usually provided from a unified department, often called a "social work department," but division into children, adult, and offender services is fairly common. Adult offenders elsewhere are dealt with mainly by the probation service, which is part of a national offender management service, including prisons and other correctional services.

Some social workers are employed by voluntary sector organizations, which are also called "third sector" or "not-for-profit" organizations. There is a great variety of different types of organizations, both local and national. Social workers also may be employed in health-care organizations, which usually are part of the National Health Service, although some National Health Service bodies have social workers who are employed by the local council and outposted to them. Many social care services are provided by private sector or for-profit organizations; these generally focus on fairly concrete residential, day, or home-care services, particularly for older people, but also for other groups with long-term conditions. There is not much private practice, but some private practitioners with a social work background provide counseling and psychotherapy; they usually are also qualified in the particular therapy and would not promote themselves as social workers. Social work is thus seen by the public largely as a local government profession. Private practice social workers also provide training and management consultancy, act as *locum tenens* social workers working through specialized employment agencies, and provide reports about children in legal proceedings on contract through the local offices of the Children and Family Court Advisory and Support Service.

Social policy derives from national debate, centered on the UK Parliament at Westminster in London, so the English system is often influential in setting policy. Most social work concerns are dealt with by the English Department of Health for adult social care, and the Department of Children, Schools and Families for children and family services. However, each separate country has its own policies and may well have a party or coalition in power of a different political complexion from the UK Parliament. This leads to different emphases in the organization of services in each UK nation.

There is a clear distinction in the UK between social workers and clinical psychologists, counselors and psychotherapists. Social work is not considered a form of counseling or psychotherapy by practitioners in those fields, and most social workers would see themselves as using counseling skills in their work rather than as practicing counseling as a profession. These professions are registered with various private bodies, but plans are being made for them all to be regulated by the Health Professions Council, a government agency. Some social workers, particularly those working in health-care settings, are dual qualified, usually training for a counseling or psychotherapy qualification after having gained social work registration, which strengthens their applications if they want to work in jobs that contain a high proportion of such work.

LOCATE LEGAL REGULATION OF SOCIAL WORK.

Regulation of social work distinguishes three main elements: professional regulation, service regulation, and knowledge development. In each country, the legislation, which dates from 2000, established one organization to regulate the quality of services and another to regulate the workforce, including social workers. There also are organizations whose role is to promote improved knowledge within social care and to enable services to use the best evidence available as the basis for their work. The relevant organizations for each of the UK countries are set out in table 3.1. In addition to these, the Office for Standards in Education assesses the quality of services for children and family provided by local authorities.

The service regulators maintain an inspection regime for all bodies that provide social care services, including residential care, day care, and domiciliary services. Local councils are evaluated annually by the Audit Commission, according to performance indicators established by the relevant government department. Councils, like hotels, are awarded a number of stars for their services, from none to three, three being those assessed according to the criteria as providing the best services. Social care services are also given a star rating. Individual care homes and other social care services complete self-assessment evaluations and are inspected; there is a program of regular visits and there also may be unannounced visits.

TABLE 3.1 LEGAL SOURCES OF SOCIAL WORK REGULATIONS

COUNTRY	LEGISLATION	REGISTRATION BODY	SERVICE REGULATOR	KNOWLEDGE DEVELOPMENT BODY
England	Care Standards Act 2000	General Social Care Council (GSCC)	Care Quality Commission (CQC)	Social Care Institute for Excellence (SCIE)
Northern Ireland	Health and Personal Social Services Act (Northern Ireland) 2001	Northern Ireland Social Care Council (NISCC)	Regulation and Quality Improvement Authority (RQIA)	Social Care Institute for Excellence (SCIE)
Scotland	Regulation of Care Act (Scotland) 2001	Scottish Social Services Council (SSSC)	Scottish Commission for the Regulation of Care (SCRC; The Care Commission)	Institute for Research and Innovation in Social Services (IRISS)
Wales	Care Standards Act 2000	Care Council for Wales (CCW)	Care Quality Commission (CQC)	Social Care Institute for Excellence (SCIE)

Reports on the visits must be provided by service providers to enquirers; these reports are available on the Internet on the website of the Care Quality Commission (http://www.cqc.org.uk/). An aspect of the inspection regime is to ensure that appropriate people are appointed to management positions and are employed by these organizations. A social work service would be expected to employ an appropriate number of qualified social workers and other social care staff with appropriate experience and other qualities.

The professional regulator operates registration and disciplinary processes for practitioners in social care. The only registered groups at present are social workers and social work students; the care councils are working toward registration of other groups during the next few years. From April 1, 2005, the term "social worker" has been a protected title under s61, Care Standards Act 2000: nobody may call himself or herself a social worker or similar job title with intention to deceive others, unless that person is registered.

IDENTIFY THE PURPOSE OF SOCIAL WORK REGULATION AND THE FORMAL DEFINITION OF PRACTICE.

The role of the professional regulators is set out in the legislation establishing the England Council, as follows; the legislation for other countries in the UK is similar. They should promote (a) high standards of conduct and practice among social care workers; and (b) high standards in their training (Care Standards Act, 2000, 54:2).

This refers to all social care workers—that is, people who might be employed providing social care. The definition of such workers includes social workers, but extends farther than those professionals. It is as follows:

"Social care worker" means a person . . . who—

(a) engages in relevant social work (referred to in this Part as a "social worker");

(b) is employed at a children's home, care home or residential family centre or for the purposes of a domiciliary care agency, a fostering agency or a voluntary adoption agency;

(c) manages an establishment, or an agency, of a description mentioned in paragraph (b); or

(d) is supplied by a domiciliary care agency to provide personal care in their own homes for persons who by reason of illness, infirmity or disability are unable to provide it for themselves without assistance. (Care Standards Act, 2000, 55:2)

The term "social care work" is defined by referring to the functions of agencies; one example of the list is "a person engaged in work for the purposes of a local authority's social services functions, or in the provision of services similar to services which may or must be provided by local authorities in the exercise of those functions" (Care Standards Act, 2000, 55:3[a]).

"Social work" is not defined in the legislation: "'Relevant social work' means social work which is required in connection with any health, education or social services provided by any person" (Care Standards Act, 2000, 55:4).

So, something becomes social work if the employer requires something to be done and chooses to see it as social work. However, the Care Council is required by s56 to maintain separate registers for social workers, and for designated groups of other social care workers, and then by s57 to decide on rules for registering people in each category, so these rules distinguish social workers from other social care workers. The legislation specifies general requirements, which give a right to registration where someone who meets them applies:

If the Council is satisfied that the applicant—

(a) is of good character;
(b) is physically and mentally fit to perform the whole or part of the work of persons registered in any part of the register to which his application relates; and
(c) satisfies the following conditions,

it shall grant the application, either unconditionally or subject to such conditions as it thinks fit; and in any other case it shall refuse it. (Care Standards Act, 2000, 58:1)

The "physically and mentally fit" criterion is controversial: it has been seen as discriminatory, since it might exclude people with disabilities or those suffering from a mental illness from registering as social workers. There are two conditions for registration (required by subsection 58:1(c) reprinted above). The first is "he [sic; UK legislation refers to one gender as including the other] has successfully completed a course approved by the Council under section 63 for persons wishing to become social workers" (Care Standards Act, 2000, 58:2a[i]). The second condition is anything else specified by the council in its rules. Therefore, in effect, whether someone is a social worker is defined by the definition of an approved course. Section 63 of the Care Standards Act permits the council to make rules for, among other things, "the content and methods of completing a course" and for the people "who may participate in courses." That means it can set criteria for entry to the profession.

However, the act also reserves a power for the government to specify the content of courses by the following provision:

The appropriate Minister has the function of—

(a) ascertaining what training is required by persons who are or wish to become social care workers;

(d) drawing up occupational standards for social care workers. (Care Standards Act, 2000, 67:1; missing paragraphs are about finance)

To understand the definition of a social worker, we therefore have to turn to the current ascertainment by the minister. This is published (Department of Health, 2002) and available on the Internet. Two crucial paragraphs require course providers to

> Design the content, structure and delivery of the training to enable social work students to demonstrate that they have met the national occupational standards for social work and the social work benchmark statement and are suitable for admission to the General Social Care Council register of social workers;
>
> and
>
> Ensure that the teaching of theoretical knowledge, skills and values is based on their application in practice. (Department of Health, 2002, 3)

The first of these paragraphs refers to two other documents; in referring to these documents the minister incorporates into the ascertainment the two significant interests in the content of social work education and the definition of social work. These two interests are the employers of social workers, who led the creation of the national occupational standards; and the educators, leading representatives of whom created the benchmark statement for the Quality Assurance Agency for Higher Education. These documents also are available on the Internet, and are very lengthy and detailed (TOPSS UK Partnership, 2002; Quality Assurance Agency, 2008). The National Occupational Standards are being revised at the time of writing, and readers may see updates on the progress of this at http://www .cwdcouncil.org.uk/nos/health-and-social-care. The second paragraph in the extract reflects the government's concern to ensure that social workers are practically competent. The document later (Department of Health, 2002, 4) sets a requirement that students must complete 1,200 hours or 200 days of practical work placement in at least two placements, one of which must incorporate practice in carrying out legal responsibilities as a social worker.

Particular "key areas" of knowledge are included in the ascertainment:

- Human growth, development, mental health and disability
- Assessment, planning, intervention and review
- Communication skills with children, adults and those with particular communication needs
- Law
- Partnership working and information sharing across professional disciplines and agencies (Department of Health, 2002, 3–4).

Of the two source documents, the National Occupational Standards refer to social care, and so do not specify a definition of social work. However, the Quality Assurance Agency benchmark discusses the definition of social work, as follows:

> Contemporary definitions of social work as a degree subject reflect its origins in a range of different academic and practice traditions. The precise nature and scope of the subject is itself a matter for legitimate study and critical debate. Three main issues are relevant to this.
>
> - Social work is located within different social welfare contexts. Within the UK there are different traditions of social welfare (influenced by legislation, historical development and social attitudes) and these have shaped both social work education and practice in community-based settings including residential, day care and substitute care. In an international context, distinctive national approaches to social welfare policy, provision and practice have greatly influenced the focus and content of social work degree programmes.
> - There are competing views in society at large on the nature of social work and on its place and purpose. Social work practice and education inevitably reflect these differing perspectives on the role of social work in relation to social justice, social care and social order.
> - Social work, both as occupational practice and as an academic subject, evolves, adapts and changes in response to the social, political and economic challenges and demands of contemporary social welfare policy, practice and legislation. (Quality Assurance Agency, 2008, 6)

To sum up this account and examine its implications for the definition of social work in regulation and licensing: rather than specify precisely what social work is in a legalistic way, the British approach is to say that a social worker is someone who has been through a recognized process of education and learning to practice. This process is defined by participation in an approved course, which should incorporate critical debate about social work's nature and contribution to society and accept a broad view of its scope. A social worker is defined, therefore, as someone who has the capacity and academic knowledge to be accepted on a university social work course and engage in such debate reflecting a range of views and competencies. By looking at the various documents discussed here, we can see what sorts of things they should be able to do and what kinds of knowledge and skills they should have developed. This is a postmodern approach to deciding what a social worker is: it is someone whose education (thinking about and doing social work) has engaged that person in the discourse about social work.

CITE THE CLASSIFICATION SYSTEM AND CLARIFY COVERAGE.

Three groups of people are currently registered:

- Social workers,
- Social work students, and
- Social workers trained and qualified outside the UK.

There is a separate application process for each group, but each is similar to the other.

EXPLAIN ANY EXEMPTIONS AND ELABORATE.

There are no exemptions; agencies may not employ someone other than a registered social worker in a post that is designated "social work" or is titled in such a way that the postholder would be taken to be a registered social worker. At present, until registration of other social care workers is completed, a variety of other job titles such as "care worker" are not included in the registration scheme.

NOTE WHAT APPLICANTS NEED TO DO: ELIGIBILITY CRITERIA AND THE APPLICATION PROCESS.

Applicants must complete an application form; these are available on the Internet (http://www.gscc.org.uk/The + Social + Care + Register/Apply + for + registration). This form covers identifying information and certification that the applicant has completed an approved course. Applicants supply a complete job and education history. They must certify that they are not subject to any disciplinary proceedings by their employer, or requirements arising from previous disciplinary proceedings. Also, they must certify that they are not subject to any criminal proceedings. At the end of the form, applicants must give information about their physical and mental health, confirm that they will comply with the Codes of Practice (see the next section), and must set up arrangements to pay the annual fee (currently £30.00, or about $48.00). A senior manager in the applicant's agency must verify the applicant's identity and endorse the application, confirming the applicant's current employment status; there are special arrangements for people who are self-employed.

Once registered, applicants must reregister every three years, submitting a record of evidence of their postregistration training and learning. This would include courses that they have attended (most short course organizers provide a certificate for this purpose), programs of reading and reflection, and evidence of research undertaken (for example, publications). Applicants are required to undertake at least ninety hours or fifteen days of such learning during each period of three years' registration. Post-registration training and learning should benefit present employment and career progression, reflect someone's personal learning style, and use the learning opportunities as part of wider professional development. The form requires applicants to specify what they have done and show how it meets these objectives. These requirements are not particularly demanding, but they do permit flexibility of learning, by enabling programs of reading to be included, for example. There is so far no provision for accrediting courses as suitable for social work postregistration training and learning, although points systems are used for medical, nursing, and legal postregistration training and learning. It seems likely that the social work system will be toughened up over the years.

Also, arrangements for postqualification education are developing strongly at present, and this is likely to provide, at least in the early stages of a career, for a fairly clear pathway of developing learning and qualification. This would lead to a master's-level qualification, since the qualifying course is set at bachelor's level, although about 20 percent of people registering as social workers do another first degree and then complete a qualifying master's-level course. Postqualification learning would take such applicants on to a more specialized master's degree program.

Applicants for registration who have completed their social work education in another country follow a similar process, and the Care Council determines whether their course is equivalent to a British course. Since most social work education around the world covers rather similar academic content and since the government is not so concerned about academic content but rather about competence to engage in the practical tasks of being a social worker, the issue often turns on the extent of supervised practice in a course. This has become an issue because the style of social work course used in the English-speaking world includes practice learning organized and evaluated by the academic institution and supervised by a fieldwork teacher in an agency. However, European courses have social science teaching that is much more extensive than is typical in the UK, but do not include supervised practice, which is often extremely limited, is not supervised, and is either part-time employment or voluntary work. Non-UK applicants without supervised practice are often required to undertake supervised practice before their qualification is recognized. Courses based in North America are usually acceptable.

SUMMARIZE STANDARDS OF CONDUCT OR PRACTICE AND THE DISCIPLINARY OR COMPLIANCE PROCESS.

Standards of conduct are specified by the care councils' codes of practice (General Social Care Council, 2004), which applicants for registration must promise to obey; they are widely published and available on the Internet (http://www.gscc.org.uk/codes). They are in the process of being rewritten at the time of this writing, and are likely to be strengthened. There are two codes: one for practitioners and one for employers. The requirements of employers include enabling their employees to comply with the employees' code and to permit and provide postregistration training and learning. The requirements of employers are generalized: they are not directed at providing an environment for good or ethical practice, but rather at more routine compliance with employers' responsibilities. They are not enforceable by law, but there are suggestions that this should change.

The employees' code also provides for some basic requirements, as follows:

Social care workers must
- protect the rights and promote the interests of service users and caregivers;
- strive to establish and maintain the trust and confidence of service users and caregivers;
- promote the independence of service users while protecting them as far as possible from danger or harm;
- respect the rights of service users while seeking to ensure that their behavior does not harm themselves or other people;
- uphold public trust and confidence in social care services; and
- be accountable for the quality of their work while taking responsibility for maintaining and improving their knowledge and skills.

More-detailed descriptions of what these headline statements mean are included, but the requirements are poorly defined and undemanding, compared with, for example, the well-established code of ethics of the British Association of Social Workers (2002).

Compliance processes are organized by the care councils; again, the English process is typical. It relies on delegated legislation (that is, the law permits the General Social Care Council to make the rules). The present arrangements are specified in the General Social Care Council (Conduct) Rules 2008, available on the Internet (http://www.gscc.org.uk/NR/rdonlyres/67F9C9D2-DE3E-4287-927C-C987911EB29D/0/2008GSCCConductRules.pdf).

These allow for the council to ask a preliminary proceedings committee to take urgent action to suspend a member of the register for six months while possible misconduct is investigated; the period can later be extended to two years. A conduct committee may then consider allegations of misconduct and order further suspension or removal from the register; a later committee may consider restoration to the register. These committees are formed from a pool of fee-paid members recruited through press advertisements. Each committee considering individual cases typically contains three members, although there may be up to five, and there must be a majority of "lay" members—that is, people not on the register. The committee must be chaired by a layperson, and a legal adviser must be present.

The procedure is this: where the care council receives information about people on the register, it must decide whether these are complaints and whether there is a case against those people that might succeed; if so, a committee is convened and a hearing takes place. Conditions—for example, additional training—may be imposed before restoration to the register is permitted. Complaints may come from members of the public and service users (the official British term for what in many countries are called "clients"), from employers, and from higher education institutions—that is, schools of social work. Most complaints are about criminal offenses or misconduct that in some way breach the trust between practitioners and service users. Current procedures have been found inadequate for dealing with public protection and quality of practice. In 2009, a large backlog in disciplinary cases in the England General Council for Social Care was identified. After an inquiry, the chief executive was fired. While there were administrative problems, the inquiry also identified problems with the legislation and rules for conducting disciplinary proceedings because they focused on identifying misconduct rather than positively protecting the public and facilitating the promotion of good practice (Council for Healthcare Regulatory Excellence, 2009).

There is little basis for dealing with allegations that might refer to poor practice, since there are few specified standards that a complainant might refer to. Most complaints of bad practice are likely to go to employers, managers, or the regulators of services; if this then leads to disciplinary action against a worker, it might be referred to the care councils for action. However, there is potential for further development among the knowledge agencies, in particular the Social Care Institute for Excellence. Although its main focus has been in producing knowledge reviews in particular areas of social work, there are some publications of guidelines that are drawn from groups of experienced practitioners and that review the nature of good practice in particular fields. If these were to become more comprehensive and authoritative, they might be used to test whether a practitioner in a good practice complaint had followed accepted practice. Currently, the only guidance would be legislation and the policies and procedures of the agency that employed the practitioners who were the subject of the complaint. However, the equivalent health-care body, the National Institute for Health and Clinical Excellence, produces extensive documentation of good practice, which is used, for example, to decide whether the National Health Service will use or finance particular medications, or treatment practices. Social work knowledge is a long way from this degree of clarity, but the UK structure makes this way of examining good practice a long-term possibility. These arrangements are typical of the provision for most other professions in the UK, in particular those in the health-care professions.

EXAMINE STRENGTHS AND WEAKNESSES OF CURRENT REGULATION; IDENTIFY ALTERNATIVE STRATEGIES.

Since most British social work is carried out within and for government agencies, the government has taken an important role in establishing professional regulation of social workers (Payne, 2007b). This assertion of a regulatory role also reflects an interventionist approach by the British government to professional regulation in other public service sectors. There are a number of reasons for this attention to government regulating professions. One is that the present government has been pursuing a public choice agenda for public services that encourages systems that enable the public to choose which services they use. Such policies require robust information to enable service users to make their choice, and to regulate the organizations so they can be sure they are performing adequately. The whole process of regulation is seen as providing accredited services in a mixed economy of care, with service providers in different sectors of the economy between which the public can choose; professional regulation is seen as part of that process.

Alternative strategies would be for professional self-regulation and employer regulation. The British state has moved away from self-regulation, which is seen to lack independence from producer interests. Self-regulating professions are seen as tending to aggrandize their status and develop their economic power so as to maintain the status quo of their own position and services; in doing so they may become unresponsive to public opinion and complaint. As a character in act 1 of George Bernard Shaw's play *The Doctor's Dilemma* says, "All professions are conspiracies against the laity." Successive British governments have argued for this position, partly to increase their own control over policy and service development. The introduction of parent governors into state schools, state control of the school curriculum on the French model, and regular inspections of schools have been partly to reduce teachers' control over the curriculum, which was seen to be excessively left-wing or socially liberal, and contrary to the economic interests of industrial and commercial development.

Another reason for this trend is public dissatisfaction with particular professions. Medical and legal scandals and the failure of self-regulatory bodies to make a robust response have played into this trend. Employer regulation had been the approach to the social services until the 1990s, and has been displaced for two reasons. Policy makers came to believe that it was inappropriate in the long term for elected local politicians to have a major role in determining the nature and role of a profession operating nationally, partly because of a long-term shift to highly centralized government, which over recent decades has left the UK among the most centralized states in Europe, if not in the world. Also, as the public choice agenda has become more important, government has accepted the force of private sector providers' arguments against their local governments, their competitors in providing services, also having the role of regulating them.

The approach to social work in the system is notably flexible. The lack of a formal legal definition of social work plus acceptance that the professional social worker and profession itself will change and develop is both an advantage and a limitation. On the one hand, this lack prevents fossilization and allows for professional developments and changing social trends to have influence. On the other hand, it permits cultural trends or press hysteria about some aspect of services, such as child neglect or abuse, to color the role of social work as the British state sees it. This lack of definition plus evolution of the profession also results in the failure to distinguish between the professional activity of social work, with its independent discretion and university-level education, from less complex work in the social care sector. The social care focus of the codes of practice, as compared with the social work codes of ethics available, suggests how the present regulatory function oversimplifies what the professional activity of social work is all about, as compared with other social care roles. In this way, social work in the UK has failed to assert an independent professional status aligning itself with leading professions. Instead, it is very much a local government professional grouping with less social status than, for example, medicine, with its powerful level of independent discretion. It also has failed to achieve the public support that nursing has achieved and still retains through sentimental regard for its role in close personal care tasks.

EVALUATE ACTUAL AND POTENTIAL IMPACTS OF CURRENT REGULATION AND PROPOSED ALTERNATIVES.

The present British system of professional regulation of social work is new; since it was resisted for many years by previous governments, most British social workers and agencies are simply grateful that it exists. Policy makers, educators, practitioners, service users, regulators, and the public at large through political representation are building up the system of social work regulation, so there is a possibility of incremental improvement. This is particularly true as postregistration training and learning develops a more stringent accreditation system and the knowledge bodies gain influence and credibility. These developments hold out hope for a stronger focus on good quality of practice.

However, the governmental focus of the organization and legal mandate emphasizes external independence in the regulation of the profession, but conversely also permits naive ignorance about the possibilities and standards that social work might offer. An example is the alternative European form of social work, social pedagogy, whose perspective has been of interest to UK social workers for many years (Haydn Jones, 1994; Lorenz, 1994; Shardlow & Payne, 1998). However, its rediscovery through government-supported research has led to a proposal to import a large number of European pedagogues to reform children's residential care. Press reports of this innovation present it as though UK ignorance of it was a failing of the imagination of the social work profession rather than of the limited perspective of government-approved service provision.

The UK system regulates practitioners as individuals while applying much less legal force to the requirements on employers to foster and sustain good practice. Lobbying by the social work profession around the redrafting of the codes of practice partly focuses on the need to balance independent professional responsibility with local and central government responsibility for providing the resources and support for good practice. It seems likely that this balance of professional and government responsibility will be increasingly needed in the future, since the next few decades will see increasing pressure on government finance of public services, coming from present economic difficulties and a rapidly increasing elderly population, which are likely to increase demands on the social care services.

An overall assessment of the regulation of social work and social care services in the UK is that there had been good progress over the past decade, but that a lot more remains to be done if social work is to be enabled to achieve as much as it could for the people of the UK.

Social Work Regulations in Selected Nations in Asia
Monit Cheung, PhD, LCSW

Regulating social work as a profession through licensure is not new in developed countries but is a concern in most developing Asian countries due to lack of resources to support licensure's legal process and implementation. In order to protect consumers and increase creditability of social work practice, eight Asian countries have publicly recognized registration, certification, or licensure laws in governing social work practice. This section describes the process of obtaining information from Asian countries and summarizes the major components of social work regulations in China, Hong Kong, Japan, Korea, the Philippines, Singapore, Taiwan, and Thailand. Social work as a profession must consider the cultural relevancy of implementing licensure in developing countries where lack of resources to support quality control is an obstacle in service delivery.

Increasingly, social workers who work globally must practice under legal protection to ensure service quality and enhance consumers' confidence. It is essential to examine how social work regulations are established in other countries so that cross-cultural practice can be connected and enhanced. Recent literature has addressed social work regulations and licensure in the United States because that entire country embraces social work licensure. Nevertheless, many countries have a long history of implementing legal regulations to protect the social work profession and its clientele. For example, in the United Kingdom a social worker must register with the General Social Care Council before performing any social work duties (General Social Care Council, 2009). In Canada, social work regulations are governed by the various Canadian provincial social work regulatory bodies and associations, depending on where the service is provided (MedHunters, 2009). Although the standards and requirements vary by country and by state within a country, all licensure laws require applicants to pass an examination that demonstrates knowledge and skills with an emphasis on theory application, professional ethics, communication skills, and cultural competency. The recognized status of a social worker is given when the work is completed with a determined level of care and skill governed by a professional body.

Globalization and the Need to Summarize Licensure Requirements in Asia

With globalization being an important aspect of social work practice, many social workers are now working away from their homelands; in particular, many are serving Asian countries, especially those with increasing challenges in social and political justice, to gain multicultural and global practice perspectives. A study by Teasley and colleagues (2005) shows that social work licensure significantly correlates with culturally competent practice. However, there is no coordinating effort that centralizes the licensing requirement information of social work for the professionals who want to practice outside Canada, Europe, or the United States. Licensure information in Asian countries will help social workers who want to work in those countries to coordinate efforts to professionalize social work, find a model to enhance qualified practice, and link qualified individuals to work in human services.

With the intention of summarizing licensing requirements in Asian countries, the author of this section (Dr. Cheung) conducted a literature search to examine social work licensure or regulation laws developed and implemented in Asian countries. However, no literature that Cheung found has addressed or summarized social work regulation information in Asia. As a result, Cheung used Internet resources to facilitate the search, and found that social work licensure with strict requirements on education, training, and examination is implemented in Korea and Taiwan. Social work certification and registration—both of which serve a similar function as licensure except for its monitoring process—are implemented in China, Hong Kong, Japan, the Philippines, Singapore, and Thailand. In Singapore, as of April 1, 2009, a newly established social work board accredits social workers, conducts renewal of social workers' accreditation, and handles complaints, as well as reviewing and approving training and continuing education (IFSW, 2009).

Internet information about social work regulations is available only from nine Asian countries: China, Hong Kong, Japan, Korea, the Philippines, Singapore, Taiwan, and Thailand. (India is included for comparison purposes in this analysis and also is covered separately in the next section.) This limited information provides an impression that licensing requirements may not be a top priority of policy implementation in many Asian countries where social services are still in a developing stage. In addition, although Hong Kong is part of China, its legal process is different from that in mainland China, and therefore its social work registration requirements are summarized separately from the mainland.

Using LICENSEE to Summarize Social Work Regulations in Asia

Using the model of analysis developed for this book (LICENSEE), Cheung collected the materials from websites that describe the social work profession in nine Asian countries. One limitation of using the Internet as the data collection method is that it may not cover all the countries that have implemented social work regulations if the country does not place information online. In addition, most websites publish information in the native language without English translation. Cheung required translation assistance in order to identify the essential components so that a summary could be provided for reference. In addition, many countries use the term "registration" to describe their regulation process and implementation but also include a certificate as the indicator that applicants have met the registration requirements including passing a public examination. To use their terminology, "registration with certificate" is the regulation category in two countries: China and the Philippines.

Seven categories of information representing the LICENSEE model are summarized below (tables 3.2 and 3.3). This research process and analysis led to three major findings that support the use of legal regulations to protect social work as a profession, help consumers identify qualified social workers, and develop strategies for social workers to commit to ethical standards of social services in further affirming social work's status as a profession. These findings are as follows:

1. Requirements: The qualification of a social worker is determined by education, training, and examination. Even though standards that adopt examination and higher education in social work are set in most countries, the levels of regulation vary. For example, China has three levels of social workers; the third level (Advanced Social Workers) must fulfill the requirements of having a social work degree, having four years of experience postundergraduate degree or one year of experience postgraduate degree, and in both cases passing a national examination. According to the regulation standards, the applicant will obtain a certificate, but the process is called "registration" and not "certification."

2. Professional identity: The identity of a social worker is correlated with the establishment of a professional association for social workers. All these nine Asian countries have established national organizations for social workers. The legal regulation of the profession is aimed at strengthening social workers' professional identity and protecting the quality of service delivery through the professional organization as a governing body. Codes of ethics become the guideposts of social work practice standards.

3. Professional responsibility: In the descriptions of the legal regulations, all nine countries require that social workers demonstrate

their work according to professional standards. Since advocacy work and membership network are generated from the country's professional organizations, a certificate or license is used as a means to show pride in taking part in the social work profession. Annual professional meetings facilitate networking opportunities and exchange of practice ideas and wisdom.

Among the Asian countries in this study, no research has been disseminated that provides evaluative data to demonstrate the connection between regulation of practice and regulation's impact on service quality, client protection, and professional image and protection of that image. It is important to first identify how the title and its legal requirements are related to the mission of the legislation, duties of the social work professional organization(s) established in the country, and the strengths and limitations of imposing regulations on the profession and its clients. In some of these nine Asian countries where social services are still in the developing stage, resources are insufficient to produce a wide range of services to improve the well-being of the individuals and families. "Protecting the profession" is not used as the only strategy to get regulation laws passed; the development of social work must be connected to the needs of its people. The use of a people-oriented approach will make the regulation work. "Putting people first" is the social work goal for the establishment of legal regulation in these Asian countries.

Future research must take into consideration how a country may use the first two levels of profession regulation (registration and certification) to pass the test of public recognition. Social work licensure does not seem to be a popular policy in Asia. Researchers must examine the cultural implications of regulating the profession of social work in countries where the priority is delivering services to meet basic needs. Licensure regulation with strict requirements and a fee-based examination may systematically exclude workers who are poor and have not received higher education locally or abroad from entering the profession. Regulations should be used to protect the profession and people using its services, and not used to exclude those who want to serve but who lack the resources to obtain a social work degree. Providing educational opportunities to train qualified social workers in Asia to work in the local context is an urgent priority.

TABLE 3.2 LICENSEE FRAMEWORK FOR ASIAN NATIONS

ELEMENTS IN SOCIAL WORK REGULATION		CHINA
L	*Type of legal regulations*	Registration with certificate (September 1, 2006).
I	*Purpose of regulation; definition of social work practice*	To monitor the professional behavior; enhance the ability; and build up the team of professional social workers.
C	*Classification, coverage*	• Junior Social Worker • Social Worker • Advanced Social Worker
E	*Exemptions*	Not specified.
N	*Eligibility, application*	To become a junior social worker or social worker upon registration: • Completed high school or higher education, • graduated from social work related education, and • passed the National Examination for Social Workers after being engaged in personal care-related occupation for one year or longer.
S	*Disciplinary standards, compliance process*	If the social work certificate is obtained illegally, a candidate cannot take the exam within two years; other misconduct will be determined by the certificate issuing agency.
E	*Strengths or weaknesses*	As a beginning milestone to mark the establishment of social work regulations, social workers' education credentials are mainly developed from Hong Kong and other countries.
E	*Impacts on the profession*	Starting to receive social and public recognition.

TABLE 3.2 LICENSEE FRAMEWORK FOR ASIAN NATIONS (CONTINUED)

HONG KONG, S.A.R.	INDIA
Registration (June 30, 1997).	Registration (proposed in 2007).
Use a regulatory system to monitor the quality of social workers and ultimately protect the interests of service users and the general public.	For the promotion, maintenance, and coordination of standards of education, training, research, and practice.
Registered Social Worker (RSW).	Registered Social Worker (proposed).
Satisfy the Social Worker Registration Board that the applicant has occupied a social work post no later than 31 March 1982; (1) subsequent to that date, occupied a social work post or posts for not less than ten years, whether or not continuously; (ii) unless the applicant satisfies the board that (a) he/she currently occupies a social work post or has been accepted for such a post; (b) if the applicant is not registered, the applicant proposes to obtain a recognized degree or diploma in social work within a reasonable period.	Not specified.
The applicant is the holder of a degree or diploma in social work recognized by the board for the purposes of this subsection.	Minimum standards have been proposed to include educational credentials and examination to be recommended by the proposed council.
Title and qualification protection.	Not specified.
Not stated.	Still in the proposal stage.
Recognized as a profession.	If the law passes, social work will be recognized as a profession and social work qualifications will be publicly recognized.

TABLE 3.2 LICENSEE FRAMEWORK FOR ASIAN NATIONS (CONTINUED)

ELEMENTS IN SOCIAL WORK REGULATION		JAPAN
L	Type of legal regulations	Certification (1998).
I	Purpose of regulation; definition of social work practice	Protect service quality that social workers can provide consultation, guidance, and other forms of support according to expertise to those who have difficulties in living their daily life due to physical/mental disabilities or environmental reasons.
C	Classification, coverage	Certified Social Worker.
E	Exemptions	Not specified.
N	Eligibility, application	(a) Completed studies in social welfare designated by the Minister for Health, Labour and Welfare in colleges and other institutions; (b) passed the National Examination for Certified Social Workers; and (c) completed the registration.
S	Disciplinary standards, compliance process	Not specified.
E	Strengths or weaknesses	Registration is the first step before taking the required examination. However, it is unclear what the legal title is if a "registered" social worker fails the examination.
E	Impacts on the profession	Social work expertise is being recognized.

TABLE 3.2 LICENSEE FRAMEWORK FOR ASIAN NATIONS (CONTINUED)

KOREA	PHILIPPINES
Certification and licensure (2003).	Registration with certificate (June 19, 1965).
To regulate and monitor the quality of social workers and protect the interests of the general public.	No person shall practice or offer to practice social work in the Philippines as defined in the Republic Act No. 4373, or be appointed as a social worker or to any position calling for social worker in any social work agency whether private or government without holding a valid certificate of registration as a social worker issued by the Board of Examinees for Social Workers.
• 1st level: passed licensing exam. • 2nd level: took required courses. • 3rd level: trained for 12 weeks.	Social Work Certificate of Registration (for both title and practice protection).
Not specified.	Exemption is used in the law but the content of exemptions is not specified.
(a) An associate's or above degree; (b) completed required courses; and (c) passed the National Social Work Examination.	(a) Is a citizen of the Philippines; (b) at least twenty-one years of age; (c) in good health and of good moral character; (d) received a diploma, bachelor's degree, or master's degree or its equivalent in social work from an institution, college, or university duly accredited and legally constituted; and (e) completed a minimum period of 1,000 case hours of practical training in an established social work agency under the direct supervision of a fully trained and qualified social worker.
Social work practice law of Korean government.	Governed by the law in the Philippines, the Board of Social Work will exercise its power to refuse the issue of the social work certificate or revoke or suspend an existing certificate based on reasons stated in the law regarding conduct and practice standard violations.
Korean language is a requirement. All social work professional websites are in Korean language.	Similar to licensure, the registration law requires education, examination, and code of ethics compliance.
A solid professional identity for social workers has been established.	The standards of these professionals and agencies hiring social workers are governed by the law.

TABLE 3.2 LICENSEE FRAMEWORK FOR ASIAN NATIONS (CONTINUED)

ELEMENTS IN SOCIAL WORK REGULATION		SINGAPORE
L	*Type of legal regulations*	Registration (April 2004).
I	*Purpose of regulation; definition of social work practice*	Values of registration are posted on Singapore Association of Social Workers website: for the public, for social worker employers, and for social workers themselves. Definition of practice is based on IFSW's definition.
C	*Classification, coverage*	Registered Social Worker (RSW).
E	*Exemptions*	Not specified.
N	*Eligibility, application*	BSW, BA (social work), MSW, graduate diploma, CSWE, or nationally accredited BSW or graduate degree in other countries.
S	*Disciplinary standards, compliance process*	Registration ensures that qualified practitioners keep their skills and knowledge current through continuing professional education.
E	*Strengths or weaknesses*	Form a group of unified social workers through registration and membership with the same professional organization, but no title protection.
E	*Impacts on the profession*	Public recognition.

TABLE 3.2 LICENSEE FRAMEWORK FOR ASIAN NATIONS (CONTINUED)

TAIWAN, R.O.C.	THAILAND
Licensure (1997).	Licensure (2009).
Protect the use of "social worker" as a professional title; improve the qualities of social work services and develop the social work profession.	Govern practice in social work.
Social Work License.	Licensed Social Worker.
Not specified.	The existing social work staff who want licensure can obtain training under Thammasat and Huachiew Chalermprakiet universities.
(1) Hold a required social work or related degree; and (2) pass the Social Work License examinations in six areas: case work, group work, community organization, public policy and legislation, human behavior, and social environment.	Those holding bachelor's degrees are considered social workers by licensure.
Code of ethics is used.	Not specified.
First Asian country to implement licensure, which signifies the importance of social work in this country; social workers' credentials must be evaluated in line with global standards.	Not specified.
Increase the reputation of the social work profession.	Moving to professionalization.

Social Work Regulations in India
Subhabrata Dutta and Chathapuram Ramanathan

National Historical and Cultural Context

India is the world's largest democracy and the world's second-most populous country. It has a very diverse population: India demonstrates linguistic and religious diversity. With regard to linguistic diversity, many believe that India is more linguistically diverse than Europe; more than fifty languages are spoken. With regard to religious diversity, the Indian population comprises Hindus (81.4 percent; the majority) and Muslims (12.4 percent). Other minority religions practiced amongst its population include Christian (2.3 percent), Sikh (1.9 percent), and other groups such as Buddhist, Jain, and Parsi (less than 2 percent). Practice of social work poses unique opportunities and challenges because of India's diversity.

India is a prominent nation in the global economy. Just as in other nations of the global South, development planners view delivery of social services as an integral part of enhancing the quality of life and functioning of its population. Prior to independence in 1947, the approach to social welfare was oriented toward social problems and social reform, with a special focus on structural institutional reforms. The Chinese traveler Hsuan Tsang observed in the seventh century that Indian people always planted trees to provide shade for travelers, and voluntarily dug wells for drinking water for the community. This collective orientation was reflected in the services provided. Over thousands of years, communities based on caste had welfare programs for the caste's benefits. It was an expectation that members of each caste contribute to caste funds in the form of cash, or in kind, or in labor to help other members in need. During times of calamities or crisis, the village community pooled its resources to meet the needs of the people (Ramanathan & Link, 1999).

The social work profession seeks to promote the values of human dignity and self-worth, social equity, people's participation and self-determination, democratic pluralism, local self-governance, and peaceful collaborative social dynamics. In India, this professional orientation encourages a critique of the ideologies that lead to systemic domination and marginalization of vulnerable groups because of their gender, ethnicity, age, health, economic background, and other attributes. Building on this critical analysis, the profession has developed sensitivity to and work with vulnerable groups such as children; youth; women; older persons; persons with varying sexual orientations, disabilities, or mental or terminal

TABLE 3.3 BOARDS, ASSOCIATIONS, CODES OF ETHICS, AND WEBSITES FOR EXAM OR REGISTRATION, ASIAN NATIONS

	EXAMINATION OR REGULATION BODY	SOCIAL WORKERS ASSOCIATION	CODE OF ETHICS	LICENSE EXAM OR REGISTRATION WEBSITE
China	Ministry of Civil Affairs of the People's Republic of China.	China Association of Social Work.	http://www .cncasw.org/ sgwh/shgzll/ 200710/ t20071023_2221 .htm.	Ministry of Civil Affairs of the People's Republic of China: http:// rjs.mca.gov.cn/ article/zcwj/ 200712/ 20071200007922 .shtml.
Hong Kong	Social Workers Registration Board.	Hong Kong Social Workers Association http://www.hks wa.org.hk/.	Code of Practice http:// www.swrb.org.hk/ chiasp/ draft_cop_c.asp.	Social Workers Registration Board: http:// www.swrb .org.hk/ index_eng.asp.
India	The National Council of Professional Social Work in India Bill 2007 was proposed on March 26, 2008, as the exam or regulation body.	National Association of Professional Social Workers in India http://www.nap swionline.org/.	Development of a code of ethics has been proposed as a task of the National Council of Professional Social Work in India.	Not yet established. Proposing the establishment of a National Council of Professional Social Work in India that sets minimum standard for the profession with registration of professionals. http://www .napswionline.org/ documents/ National%20 Council%20of% 20Professional% 20Social%20Work %20in%20India %20Bill-2007.pdf.

TABLE 3.3 (CONTINUED)

	EXAMINATION OR REGULATION BODY	SOCIAL WORKERS ASSOCIATION	CODE OF ETHICS	LICENSE EXAM OR REGISTRATION WEBSITE
Japan	Ministry of Health, Labour and Welfare.	Japanese Association of Certified Social Workers, Japanese Association of Psychiatric Social Workers, Japan Association of Medical Social Workers, Japanese Association of Social Workers.	http://www.jasw.jp/jaswtowa/jasw-rinri050127.htm.	Ministry of Health, Labour and Welfare: http://www.mhlw.go.jp/english/index.html http://www.mhlw.go.jp/english/wp/wp-hw/vol2/p2c6.html.
Korea	Ministry for Health, Welfare and Family Affairs of Korean Government.	Korea Association of Social Workers.	Code of ethics is posted on Korea Association of Social Workers website: http://www.kasw.or.kr/socialworker/Principle.jsp.	http://www.kasw.or.kr/.
Philippines	Board of Social Workers: www.paswi.org/v2/index.php/docman/doc_download/8-paswi-handouts.html.	Philippine Association of Social Workers, Inc.: http://www.paswi.org.	Code of Ethics: http://www.prc.gov.ph/documents/Board%20of%20Social%20Workers-CE.doc.	Board of Social Workers: http://www.prc.gov.ph/portal.asp?pid=71 http://www.prc.gov.ph/documents/SOCIAL%20WORKER%20LAW.PDF.
Singapore	Singapore Association of Social Workers and National Council of Social Service.	Singapore Association of Social Workers (SASW).	Code of Professional Ethics is posted on the SASW website. RSW Register is also posted on the SASW website.	SASW: http://www.sasw.org.sg/public/aboutregistration.htm.

TABLE 3.3 (CONTINUED)

	EXAMINATION OR REGULATION BODY	SOCIAL WORKERS ASSOCIATION	CODE OF ETHICS	LICENSE EXAM OR REGISTRATION WEBSITE
Taiwan	The Nation's Examination for Professionals and Technicians, The Ministry of Examination, Taiwan.	Taiwan Association of Social Workers: www.tasw.org.tw; National Union of Professional Social Workers Associations, Taiwan, R.O.C. (NUPSWA)	Code of Ethics (Chinese) is posted on the NUPSWA website: http://nusw .warehouse .com.tw Direct link: http://nusw .warehouse .com.tw/html/ front/bin/ ptdetail.phtml ?Part = news_ 970528.	NEPT: http://www .license.com.tw/ social-worker/ know/index .htm.
Thailand	The government.	The Social Workers' Association of Thailand.	Not specified.	http://www .thaingo.org/.

illnesses; the labor class; Dalits (persons who are considered to be outside the caste system, formerly known as untouchables); tribal and indigenous people; and others. Social work professionals identify and analyze the roles played by the socioeconomic-political systems of family, community, state, corporate sector, and mass media in society, especially in reinforcing domination and marginalization. Furthermore, social work professionals consider the influence of international institutions on legal and judicial systems, and welfare and development policies and schemes.

The social work profession in India pursues democratization of the above systems, aiming at empowerment of people to meet their rights to basic needs of food and nutrition; water and sanitation; livelihood and employment; health; housing; environmental sustainability; literacy and basic education; and relief and rehabilitation of displaced victims due to disasters such as earthquake, floods, tsunami, human trafficking, and collective violence. Therefore, Indian social work professionals strive to develop their knowledge base: they learn

- culture-sensitive methods of social change within the generalist, clinical, and community work and social action approaches of social work;
- management of governmental and nongovernmental or voluntary organizations;
- policy and program planning; and
- monitoring and evaluation.

Social workers participate in social movements, nonformal education and participatory training, and access to legal aid. Finally, they engage in advocacy and pursue public interest litigations. Furthermore, the social work educational community generates social work knowledge suitable for the indigenous contexts and situations and is engaged in integrating knowledge and action through student-centered classroom teaching and learning, fieldwork practicums, practice-based research, and cocurricular skill workshops, and in educating students for social work practice, research, administration, education, and training.

Social Work Education

Education for social work in India began in 1936 with the establishment of the Sir Dorabji Tata Graduate School of Social Work at Bombay (the school was renamed in 1944 as the Tata Institute of Social Sciences) by the House of Tatas, one of the largest private industrial and business enterprises in India. Earlier, in 1926, Clifford Manshardt, an American Protestant missionary who had graduated from the University of Chicago, founded the Nagpada Neighborhood House (similar to settlement houses). He proposed to the Sir Dorabji Tata Trust to establish a postgraduate school of social work (Ramanathan & Link, 1999). His vision was accepted by the trust, so that a social work educational institution of national stature would engage in a continuous study of Indian social issues and problems and impart education in social work to meet the emerging need for trained human power. This school subsequently influenced the direction of social work education and social research in India.

Over the past eight decades, the number of professional social work educational institutions within the university system has multiplied several times. While social service delivery had been undertaken indigenously for several thousands of years, more recently Western influence on the delivery of social service has become noticeable. As noted above, the main inspiration for establishment of social work education in India came from America, partly because the Tata Institute's founding director was an

American and partly because of the influence of the American system of graduate social work education. However, besides the U.S. tendency to focus on undertaking micro interventions, Indian social work educators emphasize an orientation toward social development, social action, and social change (Ramanathan & Link, 1999). The emerging social realities require that social service initiatives and action for social change in the area of social development be formulated and implemented, and that welfare as well as crisis intervention strategies be undertaken that require professionally qualified human power with a specialized knowledge base and skill sets. Social initiatives for development, social welfare, and social action that begin a process of change through enabling the vulnerable sections of the society to participate fully in the overall development of the country can be effective.

Thus, Indian social work education focuses on the quality of human power employed in the development of welfare institutions (both governmental and nongovernmental) and in people-oriented community-based social movements and services. As we apply the LICENSEE framework, we see the prominent role played by social work educators in the development of social work regulation in India. Readers will note that because legislation is just currently being proposed and implementation is in the beginning stages, some of the steps in the framework are condensed.

LOCATE LEGAL REGULATION OF SOCIAL WORK.

In the contemporary scene, schools of social work, the University Grants Commission (a national governing body of all educators), the Association of Schools of Social Work in India, and the Department of Social Welfare at the center (federal) and in the states, and the planning commission are systematically involved in the organization and delivery of education for the profession (Desai, 1987). In this context and in order to upgrade and enhance the quality of professional education and practice, as well as to make the profession more accountable to the public, a National Council of Professional Social Work Bill was drafted in 1993 and submitted to the University Grants Commission for enactment. The act is to be called the "National Council of Professional Social Work in India Act [with the year of enactment to be added to the title]." It will come into force on the date set by the government of India, by notification in the *Official Gazette*.

According to the draft act, it shall be the general function of the council to take, in consultation with the universities or other bodies concerned, all such steps as it may think fit for the promotion and maintenance of standards of education, coordination of social work education, training, research, and practice, and for the purpose of performing its functions under this act. Nevertheless, to date there is still no national licensure for the practice of social work.

Ten years later, in 2003, the state of Maharashtra separately drafted an act to provide for the constitution of the Maharashtra Council of Professional Social Work, in order to make the profession more accountable to the public. The council planned to aim at setting, promoting, and regulating standards for professional social work education and practice, their regulation, and the resulting recognition or derecognition of the institutions, and registration or deregistration of professionals.

IDENTIFY THE PURPOSE OF SOCIAL WORK REGULATION AND THE FORMAL DEFINITION OF PRACTICE, CITE THE CLASSIFICATION SYSTEM AND CLARIFY COVERAGE, AND EXPLAIN ANY EXEMPTIONS AND ELABORATE.

As of 2010, the two above-mentioned draft bills had been initiated to make a regulation of enrollment of a professional social work practitioner, and both are still under consideration as of 2010. The provisions regarding enrollment and registration follow. In section 14 of the National Council of Professional Social Work Bill, 1993, as a minimum standard for enrolment of individual practitioners, the act states

1. The Council shall prescribe the minimum standards for enrolment as Social Work Professional by its Regulations.
2. Every person, whose name is borne on the Register, shall be entitled to work as Social Work Educator or practise Social Work in any part of India.
3. No person other than the Social Work Professional, who possesses a recognised social work qualification, and is enrolled on the Register:
   (a) Shall hold office as social work professional or any such office (by whatever designation called in Government or in any institutions maintained by a local or other authority).
   (b) Shall practise as Social Work Professional anywhere in India.
   (c) Shall be entitled to sign or authenticate any certificate required by any law to be signed or authenticated by the Social Work Professional.
   (d) Shall be entitled to give evidence in any court as an expert under section (45) of the Indian Evidence Act, 1972, on any matter relating to professional social work provided that if a person possesses the recognised professional qualifications on the date of commencement of this Act, he/she shall

be deemed to be an enrolled social Work Professional for a period of six months from such commencement, and if the person has made an application for enrolment on the Register within such period of six months, till such application is disposed of,

(e) Contravention and penalty: any person who acts in contravention of any provision of sub-sections 14(3) (a), (b), (c), and (d) shall be punished with imprisonment for a term which may extend to one year or with fine which may extend to Rs.1,00,000/- or both.

Note what applicants need to do: eligibility criteria and the application process, and Summarize standards of conduct or practice and the disciplinary or compliance process.

One of the draft bills makes provision for registration of individual social work practice along with the regulation and maintenance of professional social work education in Maharashtra. According to section 10(d) of the Maharashtra Council of Professional Social Work Bill, professional social work must "Promote and Regulate Standards of Professional Social Work Practice through Development of a Code of Ethics for and Registration/Deregistration of Professional Social Workers." Section 2(a) in 12/13 states,

12. 'Professional Social Work Practitioner' means a person who holds the prescribed professional social work qualifications, from a recognised professional institution of social work education and is engaged in social work practice, and/ or administration.

13. 'Paraprofessional Social Work Practitioner' means a person who has undergone social work training at a certificate or diploma level, from a recognized institution for paraprofessional social work education and not at a degree level.

Examine strengths and weaknesses of current regulation, identify alternative strategies, and Evaluate actual and potential impacts of current regulation and proposed alternatives.

Social work as a profession is still struggling to get adequate recognition in India. In the larger society, the term "social work" is generally used to include almost any activity that is intended to help, restore, or promote some aspect of the physical, economic, and social well-being of individuals and groups (Nagpaul, 2005). Moreover, the basic philosophy and cultural traditions of Indian society continue to emphasize the ideals of self-sacrifice and dedication, which in turn offer protection and security to the individual within the Indian social structure. Mahatma Gandhi, the father of the Indian nation, received the old tradition of social service and influenced not only the establishment of services targeting weaker (marginalized) sections of the population, but also promoted the training of the workers on the ideals of dedication and self-sacrifice (Majumdar, 1965). Gandhian constructive work is deeply rooted in India, and continues to influence social work in one form or another. As a matter of fact, social work is still interpreted in this traditional society's ethos and is regarded as a voluntary service, actuated by a strong sense of altruism. There is a strong need, then, to establish tighter linkages between professional social work and Gandhi and social work, although many eminent professional social workers and educators are influenced by Gandhi and his philosophy.

The other professions in India such as law and medicine have shown limited acceptance of social work as a profession, but social work has not achieved widespread recognition. The total number of social workers is still not proportional to the country's population. In fact, social workers are employed in many settings that are mainly engaged in educational, administrative, and research activities. When there is no nationwide licensure for social work professionals, the social work profession relies on its own code of ethics. In this context, India is no exception; nevertheless, Indian social workers have questioned the relevance of clinically oriented Western codes for Indian community development. Consequently, Indian social workers prefer the use of the term "declaration" instead of "code" of ethics for people-centered work (Desai & Narayan, 1998).

Moreover, there are few positions that require training in professional social work as essential; therefore, even the very existence of the positions known as social work positions is at its minimum in the total occupational structure of Indian society. We have witnessed similar challenges to the social work profession in the United States, specifically, in the state of Michigan. In the 1980s, social work positions in public welfare in Michigan underwent declassification. Many trained social workers were eventually absorbed in a position that bears little relationship to social work. Twenty years later, the social work profession in Michigan, as in many other states, continues to struggle for a place at the table in shaping and formulating social policies or administering social welfare organizations.

But there is a silver lining in the scenario of professional social work in India. A strong National Association of Professional Social Work in India has been established by Indian professional social work educators and practitioners. Its membership is increasing steadily. Now social development is being carried by governmental and nongovernmental organization partnerships. The central government and state governments are emphasizing the need to employ professionally trained social workers in development projects. Institutes and universities are introducing social work courses in their curricula. During the past ten years, overseas funding for development work in India from international agencies such as the Department of International Development (UK), Swedish International Development Cooperation Agency, Ford Foundation, Bill Gates Foundation, World Bank, Water Aid, Oxfam, and so on has increased five times. Interestingly, such funded projects have given a boost to the professional social workers being employed in these projects: some funders require that the potential employees have either a BSW or MSW degree. Such initiatives have contributed to the scope of practice and opportunities available to social work professionals; while they are proving their mettle, social workers are playing a significant role in furthering the scope for the profession.

The contribution of social workers in India in the broad field of social relationships (which may result in problems of mutual adjustment between the individual and his or her environment) is made through their active and purposeful engagement with individuals (as individuals or within groups), their understanding of human behavior, their knowledge of common resources, and their ability to see individual needs within the broader perspective of social needs for effective and concerned social action. Given that Indian society's traditional value system is very significant and germane to day-to-day social transactions, the development of the profession in terms of licensing requirements is at a different stage from what it is in several Western nations and in other Asian nations that are more comfortable in adopting the Western licensing model. The proportion of voluntary social work in their respective societies may be different from what it is in Indian society. Therefore, opportunities for clinical social work practice in India are not as popular in comparison to the United Kingdom or the United States. Naturally, the scope of practice is limited for individual practice. In addition, many social work educators and practitioners are working in India as consultants, which does not require registration. The numbers of social workers working as consultants are steadily increasing because almost all development agencies hire them for their projects. Unfortunately, no official data are available regarding the number of social work consultants in India.

Thus, it will be accurate to conclude that there is ample scope for professional social work practice in India because it is a vast country with more than 1.1 billion people, and a number of governmental and nongovern-mental organization–funded agencies (including foreign funders) as well as development agencies employ trained social workers. The government of India has already recognized the expertise of the social work profession: many of its research and development projects are managed by profes-sional social workers and educators. It is anticipated that India's strong professional association (National Association of Professional Social Work in India) is likely to continue to pursue registration of professional social work practice in India and promote indigenous elements of social work education in terms of its philosophy, approaches, principles, and educa-tional materials because working with people in India, studying social problems, and administering social welfare programs require indigenous orientation and skills. (See Gunavathy, 2007, and Nanavatty, 1997, for more on the development of social work as a profession in India.)

Social Work Regulations in Mexico and Canada

Those interested in practice opportunities in either or both of the countries adjacent to the United States will encounter two different situations with regard to the status of regulation of social workers and social work practice.

Canadian policies regulating social work are more similar to the United States at this writing than are those in Mexico (Randall & DeAngelis, 2008). In the ten Canadian provinces, social work regulation is formally estab-lished. The boards that regulate social workers are members of the ASWB and some use ASWB's examinations. Information regarding the process for applying for a social work license in Canada and for other resources is available through ASWB's website (www.ASWB.org). (See the interna-tional resources in appendix B in this primer.)

Canadian social work shares similar origins as well with social work's historical development in the United States starting more than one hun-dred years ago. However, in addition to influences from English social work that were significant in the United States in the late 1800s, the devel-opment of Canadian social work tapped into social work approaches from France, Ireland, and Scotland (Turner, 1997), and social workers there have distinct and complex perspectives. Moreover, "there is a growing realiza-tion that the first-nation peoples, the original inhabitants of the country, have important contributions to make to the development of professional services in the country from the basis of their history and cultures" (pp. 30–31). The professional identity of social workers and the regulation of their practice thus are informed by both international and indigenous sources.

Applicants will find that the variations in regulations from jurisdiction to jurisdiction, state to state, province to province, in both the United States and Canada, can lead to confusion and threaten the objective of ensuring minimum standards of practice and public protection (Collins, Coleman, & Miller, 2002). Required educational background, credentials, rules, and exemptions in addition to the array of titles given social workers challenge the identity and unity of the profession. However, ASWB's model act provides an opportunity for jurisdictions to align their regulations more in tune with each other in the future; the trend in both the United States and Canada is from title protection to practice act (DeAngelis & Monahan, 2008). (For more information on Canadian social work, see ASWB's website; Turner, 1997; and other resources listed in appendix B of this primer.)

While in some ways similar to the United States and Canada, social work in Mexico is also ingenious in ways that can be inspiring as well as fascinating for students and social workers from the United States. (For informative summaries of the profession in Mexico, see Aguilar, 1997; Herrick & Stuart, 2005; and Zárate & Treviño, 2007.) Although, like Canada, historical influences on Mexican social work from models first developed in other countries including Belgium, France, Germany, and the United States are evident, the recent development of social work in Mexico shares with other Latin American countries a deep and abiding commitment to alignment with public health practitioners and to liberation philosophies (such as the teaching of Paulo Freire, 1989; see also Bibus, 1995; and Bibus & Link, 1999, pp. 104–106). There is a much more pronounced focus on group practice and community organization and development in Mexican approaches to social work in contrast to the keen attention to individual casework typical in the United States. Perhaps partly for this reason, regulation of practice is taking a more deliberate path thus far in Mexico than it has in the United States. As of this writing, the regulatory body for social workers is not a member of ASWB.

The development of regulation of social workers and their practice in Mexico has not moved beyond stipulating the educational criteria required to be met for Licenciado en Trabajo Social, which is essentially equivalent to an undergraduate degree in social work (e-mail communication, Antonio Ortega, Augsburg College Center for Global Education, January 29, 2009). "There are 24 states in the republic with at least one school or faculty of social work" (Zárate & Treviño, p. 114; see also p.105, p. 108). Once social work graduates register their degree and title of "social worker" with the

professions department of the federal government's Secretaría de Educa-
ción Pública (Ministry of Public Education), they receive a *cédula professional* (professional identification card); beyond examinations required by
the university's educational program, no additional examination, continuing education, or other documentation is required. There are two career
options for social workers, which are essentially dependent on the level of
education obtained: (1) becoming an entry-level social work technician by
completing training equivalent to high school and technical education in
the United States, and (2) becoming a professional social worker by completing five to six years of higher education, including a practicum in a
program certified by Mexico's Ministry of Public Education (e-mail communication with Dr. José Luis Luna Aguilar, Secretarío de Vinculación
Intra y Extra Institucional, September 30, 2009). Social workers at any of
the forty social work schools and in each of the thirty-two states follow
this same process for registration, so students who are looking into practicing in Mexico should begin their inquiries with the federal Ministry of
Public Education.

Summary of Global Status

In a recent comparison of the social work profession across ten countries,
Weiss and Welbourne (2007) note that the support of wider society is necessary to achieve those indicators of professionalism tied to public status
and remuneration. Among the aspects of the movement toward professionalism that require the support of wider society are "licensing regulations
and procedures, restrictions on the use of the title of 'social worker,'
monopoly over fields of practice, state sanctions for the Code of Ethics,
and control over professional training and entrance into the profession"
(p. 245).

These regulatory policies provide for community standards and set criteria for determining who is eligible and qualified to practice social work and
who can claim the title of "social worker." While countries vary globally in
the extent to which regulation of social work has developed, the trend
across nations is toward regulation that is more formal as a means of securing high-quality social work services for their people. Weiss and Welbourne (2007) conclude, "Whatever the degree of public recognition, in
most of the countries included here there is clear aspiration to attain or
extend regulation of the profession" (p. 230). This growth in regulation of
social workers and our practice remains controversial, however—in fact it
is one of the most controversial areas in the social work community today,
as we will see in the next chapter.

CHAPTER FOUR

Social Work Profession(al)-in-Environment: SW-PIE

THIS CHAPTER REVIEWS many of the tensions and debates surrounding licensing in their interconnected context so that students can critically navigate the professional environment they are preparing to enter. We will see that the challenges involved in becoming a licensed social worker often hinge on promising doors to meaningful practice and vice versa; for example, potential opportunities such as using online technologies to extend services across jurisdictions present regulation challenges. And we will note that there is room for reasonable social workers to disagree on the merits and harms arising from the intentions and outcomes of licensing.

As we noticed in the previous chapter, while social work and social work regulation have an international presence, there is also a wide array of variations around the world in the job titles, roles, expectations, demands, sanctions, rules, laws, and standards under which social workers practice. Even within a particular nation, social work regulation can vary and may not have developed uniformly across the country. Such is the case in the United States. With some exceptions—such as in civil rights, national defense, environmental health, social security, and interstate commerce—the U.S. federal system gives primacy to states' rights. Thus, although all of the states and the District of Columbia, Puerto Rico, and the Virgin Islands regulate practice, no single jurisdiction has a set of regulations that is identical to another. This lack of consistency, which NASW refers to as a "hodgepodge of licensing requirements" (2009, p. 79), presents a major challenge to the two primary purposes of licensing:

1. to set minimum standards to which social workers are accountable and

2. to provide a legal mechanism to report and have investigated

complaints that a social worker's practice falls below standards of competence or ethical conduct or that an individual is practicing without a license.

Both practitioners and clients could easily meet with confusion and frustration when moving from one state to another. They also will encounter differences in or exemptions to such standards as

- the educational preparation to be eligible to apply for licensing as a social worker;
- the fees, examinations, continuing education, and supervision required;
- the competencies needed and scope of practice regulated;
- the procedures to follow for compliance and complaints; and
- the standards of practice and conduct set in statute or rule.

(For recent descriptions of the confusing national landscape of social work licensing, see Epple, 2007, p. 272; Groshong, 2009; Randall & DeAngelis, 2008, Robb, 2004; and Sfiligoj, 2009).

Variation in regulatory policies from state to state is a good example of one of the aspects of licensing that lead to controversies and questions regarding the benefits and costs of regulating social work practice. In an attempt to address this confusion, the national Dorothy I. Height and Whitney M. Young, Jr. Social Work Reinvestment Act, which at this writing is progressing through Congress, calls for a study of social work licensure and potential reciprocity agreements for providing services across state lines (Sfiligoj, 2009). At the same time, the 2010 Social Work Congress convened by NASW and other social work associations identified licensing as one of the issues critical in the future of the profession.

These efforts to clarify professional identity and shore up a unified common ground are timely. The bewildering array of titles for social workers and inconsistencies in definitions of practice from state to state should not be surprising given the division within the profession itself. (This observation and subsequent discussion arose in conversation with Dr. Tom Meenaghan, February 9, 2010.) It is no wonder that licensing regulations are confusing; we in the profession have struggled to communicate to lawmakers a single coherent message: The future of the profession and its valuable mission is at stake. Facing competing views of what exactly social work is while facing severe budget shortfalls, political leaders may find it hard to make social work a public priority.

Social work's dual focus on people in their environments is a strength, but this dynamic perspective also brings with it a faultline that could bifurcate *person* from *environment*, widen the rift between direct services and community organizing or policy practice (or even separate clinical social work from the rest of social work—see Groshong's argument for this separation). At our best, social workers attend both to private troubles and public issues and their interaction, yet we also risk dividing into separate professions without the commonalities inherent in the historic legacy of social work principles: service, social justice, human dignity and relationships, competence and integrity (as presented in the NASW Code of Ethics). Legislators and policy makers may wonder what it is the profession wants when social workers bicker among themselves over, for instance, whether BSW practitioners' practice should be regulated through licensure or whether licensing should be reserved only for clinical practice.

As discussed by Payne and others, these tensions are potentially healthy, and reasonable arguments can be made to support distinctions in scopes of practice within social work (or *social works*); perhaps community organization and policy practice do not need the same degree of regulation for public protection as generalist direct practice and clinical practice do. Yet, in the effort to secure title protection in order to clarify who is a social worker and what then is social work practice, do we end up working at cross-purposes? When we make praiseworthy efforts to develop the workforce and support social workers in attaining advanced education, competencies, and credentials, have we inadvertently established two tiers within the profession? Does the status associated with professional licensing siphon leading practitioners off into supervisory positions or into narrowly focused clinical practice instead of continuing to devote their talents to direct helping services, generalist practice, community organizing, neighborhood development, policy practice, or advocacy?

These are the kinds of questions that we hope are raised in this chapter. As usually is true with important dilemmas, there are not likely to be simple answers, but we are confident that the process of addressing the questions will sharpen our understanding of the issues at stake and lay the foundation for a more coherent and unified message from social workers on the role of regulation in our practice and mission. Aware of the potential for bifurcation, we will use the familiar, time-tested, and coalescing perspective of person-in-environment, adapting it to frame licensing controversies as arising in the context of the *profession(al)*-in-environment. Among potentially divisive issues, we choose to discuss here the very purpose of social work regulation, the definition of social work practice, the scope of practice (dealing with the thorny distinctions between generalist and clinical practice and access to licensing for BSW practitioners), the role of a national standardized examination as a gateway to licensing and its interrelationship with accredited social work curriculums, exemptions (including whether social workers who teach social work should be licensed), the distinctions in role and function between regulatory bodies and professional associations, selected emerging issues such as tele-practice, and the basic question of evidence for effectiveness of licensing in achieving its purposes. There are other issues and questions that we encourage students to generate, explore, and discuss; the profession will be the stronger for this discourse.

We first address the broad contextual licensing issues that continue to raise questions among social workers, advocates, and policy makers, and then we move to presenting particular issues where the most controversial elements of licensure often manifest themselves. Even if a specific technical issue were resolved to the satisfaction of most social workers, the broader contextual and political tensions might still remain troubling or become even more pressing than they are now. For example, one technical debate is whether there should be evidence that a particular mode of practice sanctioned under a licensee's scope of practice is in fact effective. To address this issue, regulators might require that licensees engage only in models of practice that have met criteria to be considered "evidence based" (Adams, Matto, & LeCroy, 2009; Minnesota Department of Human Services, 2007; Surface, 2009; Walker et al., 2007). However, while licensing of practitioners trained, for instance, in cognitive behavioral evidenced-based interventions might be associated with improved mental health for older adults (see Gellis, McClive-Reed, & McCracken, 2008, for example, and Ronan & Freeman, 2007), would restricting social workers to this model lead to a narrower delineation of social work practice? Would regulation then cover only clinical practice and ignore BSW or MSW generalist case management, administration, or community practice? And if licensees show expertise in dealing with adults' mental health, does that mean they also are competent to practice with children facing mental health challenges? Should licensees be proscribed from practice with age groups unless they have demonstrated competencies with particular categories by age of client (as recommended in Minnesota Department of Human Services, 2007, p. 20). We will see that few single controversial issues exist in isolation or stand alone; rather, most are interconnected and contribute to the complexity of the environment of professional social work practice that influences each of us and that we can together influence as well.

Applying SW-PIE

Social work is known for the person-in-environment (PIE) perspective: that is, we approach each helping situation with the fundamental realization that people exist in a particular social and physical environment. The *Encyclopedia of Social Work* (Mizrahi & Davis, 2008) describes PIE as a "guiding principle that highlights the importance of understanding an individual and his or her individual behavior in light of the various environmental contexts in which that person lives and acts" (Kondrat, 2008, p. 348). The social work profession itself (including students, schools of social work, practitioners, agencies, professional associations, regulatory bodies, etc.) exists also in an environmental context, as does each social worker. Thus, what we are calling the social work profession(al)-in-environment perspective (SW-PIE) can be very useful in understanding as well as mobilizing to influence the complex regulatory landscape within which we practice (Boutté-Queen, 2009).

As shown in figure 4.1, the SW-PIE perspective goes beyond the original and individually specific definition of PIE, with which many of us are familiar. It not only takes into account individual components of the profession at every level, but it also addresses changes undertaken or experienced by the whole as a result of changes in our various environments. Furthermore, we must recognize that what makes social workers different from other people influenced by environmental components is the added responsibility of advocating for change where change is truly needed. Simply put, we bring to the table everything we are, but changing the course of the meal rests with us as professionals. This perspective is applicable in terms of education, testing, licensing, and even determining or measuring practice competence.

Licensing is involved in all the forces represented by the arrows labeled in figure 4.1. The sanction to practice and hence earn a living comes through the legislative and political processes that establish professional regulation. The profession's social status and integrity in the community are intricately involved in licensing. Thus, our professional lives are integral with social work regulation. As we will discuss further in chapter 5, licensing can be critical to the very meaning we give to the profession.

A resource for social work educators and students developed by the Minnesota Board of Social Work and its coalition of licensed social workers (composed of the professional social work associations in the state) begins by describing the environmental context within which licensed social workers practice:

> The practice of every social worker . . . is affected by the state licensing board, various state departments, the legislature, and the insurance industry.

FIGURE 4.1 SW-PIE

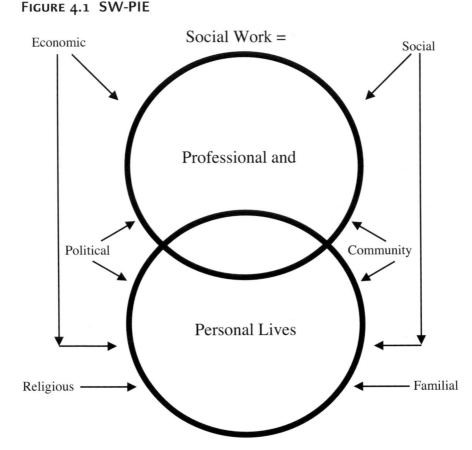

Laws, rules, reimbursement policies impact practitioners working in the private sector and public agency social workers employed by counties, cities, and the state. In addition, federal regulations further govern our practice. (Luinenburg, Zacher-Pate, Holcomb, & Bibus, 2002, p. 9)

Luinenburg and colleagues (2002) suggest an activity for students to begin thinking systemically about the regulatory environment of their practice in the same way they are learning to apply social work's dual focus on direct practice and social change in the context of their practice with clients. Students are asked to imagine an individual social worker focusing appropriately and intently on his or her work with the client system. However, as much as the social worker might prefer to be free to act in the best interests of the client, practice decisions are in fact constrained and to a major extent directed (or even controlled) by regulations and regulatory bodies that loom in the background. These bodies include legislatures and agencies at local, state, regional, and federal levels, the United Nations, courts at all levels, insurance agencies, and of course licensing boards. These sources of regulation, represent in turn only a portion of the macro-environment that influences practice and that social workers must work together with others to influence, including service agencies and their man-dates, organizations and their rules, unions and the expectations of their members, funders and their requirements, and all the other social policies that can affect practice decisions. Clearly, professional practice, with its connotations of expertise, independence, autonomy, ethical responsibility, and discretion, is not free of substantial external dictates from an ever-growing and changing regulatory system. Thus it behooves us to have this influence in mind as we practice and to continue to learn about and stay up-to-date on regulatory policies, particularly licensure.

The focus of this primer is one of these regulatory bodies: the local licensing board that governs the practice of social work licensees. As noted earlier, every state in the United States now formally regulates social work practice with legislation that functions as title protection (restricting the job title of "social worker" only to individuals who meet the requirements set forth in statute or rule, and providing sanctions against those who might call themselves "social workers" without proper licensure) or with a full-fledged practice act (setting forth minimum eligibility and practice standards, compliance and complaint processes, plus title protection). Licensure nevertheless remains one of the most controversial areas of social work practice. Gambrill and Pruger (1992) list "Should Social Work-ers Be Licensed?" as one of twenty-four controversies among social work-ers at the time and give it as an example of the cautionary note that just because something is accepted and legal does not mean it is best. (See also Epple, 2007; Holcomb, 2002; Land, 1988; Robb, 2004.) Gandy and Ray-mond (1979) summarize the earlier debates among social workers regard-ing licensing, a debate that Gross refers to as a "hot" issue (1978, p. 1009) and whose flavor is captured in some of the article titles referenced by Gandy and Raymond: "Missing the Point of Licensure," "Playing the Doz-ens," and "Licensing Battles Fought in the States."

Garcia (1990a) builds on Gandy and Raymond's (1979) work describing the support for licensing on the grounds that it gives social work legal definition, protects consumer rights, raises standards of competency, pro-vides for accountability to the public beyond the professional associations, and keeps social work comparable in status and vendor eligibility to other helping professions. He also summarizes positions opposing licensing as elitist, exclusionary, discriminatory in examinations and requirements for certain privileged educational backgrounds, an interference with market forces, cumbersome and expensive with multiple levels of licensure, and a duplication of function with CSWE's accreditation process. Garcia notes that groups such as the National Association of Black Social Workers oppose social work licensing. (For a comprehensive and coherently organized account of the development of regulation of social work in the United States, see Thyer and Biggerstaff, 1989, and their Table 2, p. 23, displaying positive and negative views of professional credentialing.) Referencing the series of publications edited by Gambrill and Pruger on controversies in social work ethics, policy, and practice in the mid-1990s that include Atherton's rejoinder to the question of whether licensing in fact protects the public from incompetent practitioners, Thyer (2010) remarks upon the continuing ambivalence within the profession toward licensure. Finally, at the beginning of the twenty-first century, the CSWE issued a rare position statement opposing mandatory licensing for social work faculty: "While the Council supports the concept of licensing in cases in which the public is directly served, it opposes efforts to utilize the licensing process in the arena of social work education" (CSWE, Fall 2001, p. 8).

Let's look at why regulation of social work practice, while established in law in every state, is still controversial among social workers.

Purpose: Protection of Professionals or Public?

At the most fundamental level, the very purposes of licensing social workers have been questioned. Skeptical critics have pointed out that the originating and strongest support of licensing provisions in the United States was organized under the auspices of NASW, its predecessor professional associations, and its local chapters. As pointed out by Gross (1978, p. 1013, and documented to be the case for social work by Thyer and Biggerstaff, 1989, among others), "[L]icensing has rarely been sought by the public; rather it has been sought by the professionals who wished to be licensed." Nevertheless, NASW and other supporters of licensing always assert that the primary purpose of licensing is protection of the public, especially consumers of social work services who are from disenfranchised groups. NASW first adopted a resolution in support of licensing in 1969 (Agostinelli, 1973). Explaining NASW's support for licensure in commentary on the 1973 revision to its model social work licensing statute, Agostinelli lists five principal rationales for licensing: "*Consumer protection . . . Sound programs . . . Quality of services . . . Career continuum . . . Responsibility of government*" (p. 4; italics in original). However, in addition to stating that regulation "offers the public the opportunity for fast and inexpensive redress for malpractice and professional dishonesty" (p. 4), he also focuses on the purpose of licensing as protecting professionals' practice.

Supporters of licensing legislation argue that by clarifying who are competent social workers, by setting standards, and by providing for "an accessible forum in which clients may raise charges of malpractice and unethical conduct, licensure raises the quality of client services" (Land, 1988, p. 94; see also Karls, 1992; NASW, 2005 and 2009, pp. 77–81; Randall & DeAngelis, 2008; and Sfiligoj, 2009). After all, according to NASW's recent study of the workforce of social workers in the United States (Whitaker, Weismiller, & Clark, 2006), social workers are "key providers to the most vulnerable populations, providing a safety net of services to older adults, neglected and abused children, and people at high risk for disparate health and behavioral health service access, treatment, and outcomes" (Executive Summary, p. 33).

In August 2008, the Delegate Assembly of NASW reiterated its support for licensing as "insurance for high quality social services and maintenance of professionalism," but it also affirmed the need for "title and practice protection through regulation for social work in all practice settings on all practice levels" (NASW, 2009, p. 79, p. 81). So, perhaps NASW's real goal in advocating for licensure is more self-serving. Might social workers who support licensing be most interested in enhancing the image, status, and prestige of their occupation compared with other licensed helping professions? Might the intent of licensing be to secure vendorship or third-party reimbursement for social work services so that social workers in private practice can compete in the market and make a more lucrative living? Might NASW be more interested in title protection than public protection? Might, as charged by Mathis (1992), licensing of social workers actually have harmful, even discriminatory and racist impacts?

> The argument may be summarized as follows: social work licensing narrows the scope and the nature of services delivered to people of color and other disadvantaged communities. Secondly, it restricts job opportunities for people of color. Moreover, by utilizing invalid and biased testing and formal, university-based education as the basic screening mechanisms for entering the profession, it limits the entry of people of color and unorthodox perspectives in the profession. Finally, it reflects an inherent political bias, serving to screen out disproportionately militant, progressive, and other nonmainstream perspectives. (p. 59)

This challenge to the core rationale for social work licensure, questioning whether regulation of social work practice is truly meant to provide a measure of safety to clients or whether instead it is meant to bolster an elite cadre of social workers and our profession, is either directly at issue or indirectly in the background in each of the controversial licensing issues that we address in the following sections. Supporters of licensing will point to the requirement that is now in many jurisdictions that licensing boards include public members as well as professional members so that professional self-interest is balanced by society's interests, but those who are skeptical toward licensure's altruistic intent suspect that public members are swayed by professional members (who often outnumber them). We will keep coming back to the question: Does licensing foster the interests of the public or the interests of social workers, or both?

Definition: What Is Social Work Practice and What Is Not?

One of the most difficult challenges for boards of social work and lawmakers is defining the broad-ranging practice of social workers with enough specificity to regulate practice without losing the essence of the profession's complex identity. State legislatures have struggled with how to operationalize the elements of social work as distinguished from the scope of practice of other licensed or unlicensed helping professionals. In the commentary on the ASWB's *Model Social Work Practice Act* (2007a), the definition of practice is called "the most important and most discussed clauses" in the model act (p. 4); the commentary goes on to explain why the recommended definition is short on specifics:

> Social work has been a very dynamic profession, particularly over the past several years, and any definition of practice needs to contain a degree of flexibility that will allow the Board to make necessary adjustments from time to time to meet a changing healthcare environment, an evolving practice, and the ongoing needs of consumers. (p. 4)

The act includes fairly general definitions for three categories of license: baccalaureate (BSW), master's (MSW), and clinical; the commentary urges boards to tailor the definitions with more specifics through the rules process, which would be sensitive to local needs and allow local input. The commentary also asserts that "social workers whose employment or position entails any or all" of the activities listed in the definitions must be licensed, including social workers in government agencies, case managers, evaluators and researchers, supervisors and administrators, community organizers and policy makers, and social work educators (p. 5). The core definition of each category states that practice "means the application of social work theory, knowledge, methods, ethics and professional use of self to restore or enhance social, psychological, or biopsychosocial functioning of individuals, couples, families, groups, organizations and communities" (p. 4). Activities listed range from assessment and intervention through supervision and policy practice. Definition of practice with the MSW license adds to generalist practice "the application of specialized knowledge and advanced practice skills" plus two activities not in the BSW list: "treatment . . . and research" (p. 6). Finally, the clinical license's definition specifies "the application of clinical knowledge and advanced clinical skills" and the additional activity of "diagnosis and treatment of mental, emotional, and behavioral disorders, conditions, and addiction" (p. 6). Specific methods of counseling and psychotherapy also are listed, as is the possibility of private practice and providing clinical supervision within the scope of practice with this license.

Most state boards have developed more detailed definitions so that what is or is not social work practice can be delineated (see ASWB's comparison guides and tables presenting social work laws and regulations for each jurisdiction, available at www.ASWB.org). Yet, establishing a clear-cut case against a practitioner who appears to be practicing social work without a license is difficult. In chapter 3, we learned that regulators in Great Britain have been adopting a strategy to make definitions more enforceable by tying the identification of who is a social worker to what the employer considers to be social work duties necessitating the hiring of a social worker. Some state boards also have tightened their definitions by linking the practice definition to social work education and to the requirements set by employers. For example, in 2009, on recommendation of the board's legal council, the Minnesota legislature added this language to the definition of social work in its practice act: "Practice of social work also means providing social work services in a position for which the educational basis is the individual's degree in social work" (MS 148D.010 Subd. 9). Thus, if a job description sets forth an expectation that the position requires the worker to have a social work degree, individuals in that position who have an accredited BSW or MSW degree must then also obtain and maintain a social work license.

Scope of Practice: Only MSW Prepared and Clinical?

Early licensing legislation in the United States did not set aside a special license for clinical practice; however, as Randall and DeAngelis (2008) point out, "the practicalities of parity with other mental health professions and the need to qualify for third party reimbursement to achieve this drove the pursuit of specific clinical social work licensure" (p. 88). Debates on social work licensure often fix on the fact that licensing appears to be primarily and in some states only available for MSW practitioners or more exclusively just for clinical practitioners, barring many other social workers from access to licensing. (We count four states that license only MSW clinical social workers and thirteen states that omit BSW social workers who do not also have an MSW degree from their licensing legislation.)

Clinical practice is of course a specialty within social work. Here is the American Board of Examiners in Clinical Social Work's definition:

> Clinical social work is a mental-health profession whose practitioners, edu-
> cated in social-work graduate schools and trained under supervision, master
> a distinctive body of knowledge and skill in order to assess, diagnose, and
> ameliorate problems, disorders, and conditions that interfere with healthy
> bio-psychosocial functioning of people—individuals, couples, families,
> groups—of all ages and backgrounds.
>
> American Board of Examiners in Clinical Social Work; retrieved on
> August 6, 2009 from http://www.abecsw.org/about-definitions-csw.html

See also the Clinical Social Work Association Code of Ethics at http://www
.clinicalsocialworkassociation.org/content/ethics-code.

Clinical social workers thus build on their generalist foundation of social work knowledge and skills to specialize in helping clients who are facing mental health or behavioral challenges. Often they practice in community clinics or medical settings on an agency's payroll, and they also may have a private practice in which they charge fees for services. Their services, sometimes categorized as psychotherapy, are usually at least partially covered under private insurance or government health-care programs such as Medicare. Both because of the vulnerability of the clientele for clinical services and because of the vendorship issues, lawmakers are persuaded more readily of the need to regulate clinical practice. Available in every state (Randall & DeAngelis, 2008; and Groshong, 2009), the clinical license is the category of licensing to which many social workers and social work students aspire even if they do not plan to pursue private practice. A recent book (Groshong, 2009) presents some of the shortcomings inherent in regulations of clinical practice as they vary from state to state and recommends improvements based on a clear identity for clinical social workers; the author argues for distinguishing clinical social work as a distinct profession, separate from social work understood as providing direct services.

As we will see below, social work educators who are not clinical social workers may not be able to be licensed in states that do not regulate generalist or advanced nonclinical practice, presenting major dilemmas when those same states move to require social work faculty to be licensed.

The issue of licensing of MSW practitioners and not BSW practitioners is intertwined with the issue of vendorship (social workers charging clients fees for service); this intersection has sparked vigorous debate over the years. Lieberman, Shatkin, and McGuire (1988) define vendorship legislation as providing "for reimbursement by insurance companies for selected services to social workers licensed at the appropriate level" (p. 59). They state that some social workers vigorously opposed such legislation on ideological grounds as antithetical to the altruistic mission of social work and as antifeminist, as well. Then they summarize the arguments in favor of vendorship legislation as a largely pragmatic mechanism for making the highest-quality social work services available to those who might not otherwise have access to them or be able to afford them. The study reported on in their article represents a rare example of an effort to gather empirical evidence to examine the assumptions behind opposition or support for this aspect of licensure. They found that in Maine, at least, vendorship legislation did contribute to an increase in the number of social workers who were able to establish a private practice as their primary work setting and that they saw more clients, improving access to mental health services in rural areas but also raising prices for those services.

Another issue related to the perception that licensure is meant primarily for MSW or clinical practitioners in private practice is the experience of African American social workers, a large proportion of whom are BSW practitioners and work in big cities where MSW programs at times dominate social work's voice in influencing licensing policies. As noted above, some social workers of color view licensing as discriminatory and oppressive to their practice. Garcia notes that "by definition, legal regulation reflects a standard of exclusivity, that is that only those who meet certain predetermined criteria should be allowed to practice in regulated areas" (1990a, p. 493). He also observes, "while the disproportionate exclusion of minorities may not be an explicit goal of legal regulation, it might be a latent effect of that process," and he reiterates the National Association of Black Social Workers' opposition at that time to licensing because it tends to exclude practitioners of color in the view of the association's membership (p. 493, pp. 496–497). However, other social workers of color will object that opposing licensing based on assumptions that they might not pass a rigorous national examination or meet other standards of educational preparation and competence is insulting if not outright racist. Nevertheless, the professionalization of social work itself, of which licensing is a manifestation, has come under critical examination over the years from radical perspectives. (See Reisch & Andrews's 2002 history of radical social work in the United States.) Some of this criticism is focused on the dominant role of standardized examinations in determining who is competent to practice social work.

The Licensing Exam: Assessment of Clinical or Social Work Practice Competency?

Much attention has been given to the concept of competence in terms of fitness to practice. As noted previously, for many years competence has been determined by the passing of a standardized examination. Middleman (1984) raises important points when stating,

> The decision about competence is inevitably a probabilistic one. That is, regardless of definition, levels, and instrumentation, whether or not the assessment process is fair for a given individual remains impossible to determine with certainty: it is a "more-or-less" question. A fair, accurate assessment can exist in principle for most candidates, but to some extent the examining experience will be "closer to home" for some. (p. 150)

Some social workers who are not clinicians (including a large number of social work faculty members) object to ASWB's examinations as focusing too much attention on testing for the knowledge, skills, and abilities needed for clinical practice and not enough attention on community or policy practice. All of the states except California, which has developed its own examination, use one or more of the standardized examinations administered by ASWB. This means that, despite the multiple variations of state regulatory policies with differing definitions of what constitutes social work practice, there is at least some uniformity in one of the measures of social work competence to which most licensees must conform. The ASWB standardized examination is thus a strength in the U.S. system of social work regulation. Nevertheless, as we discuss below, the design features that make standardized tests as reliable and valid as possible also raise questions about potential barriers to licensure of competent applicants. The examinations are revised periodically based on systematic job analyses involving a survey of practicing licensed social workers that generates a compilation of the knowledge, skills, and abilities that social workers minimally need to practice with a BSW, MSW, or clinical license. The costs involved in designing the examinations and testing their validity and reliability, reducing any bias, offering and scoring the examination, reporting results to member boards, maintaining relevant databases, and protecting the integrity of the examination content and process are borne by licensees through the fees paid to ASWB. Because of the relative affordability of designing standardized multiple-choice format examinations and their legal defensibility if candidates challenge the results of the examinations in court, at this writing ASWB examinations contain multiple-choice questions only. Test questions are generated by selected and trained licensed practitioners from across the country; the content of the examination (i.e., the competencies that are to be tested for) is updated by means of regular periodic task analysis surveys (about every seven years); questions and answers for the exam are reviewed, tested, and recommended for inclusion by an ASWB committee; and any items that psychometric evaluation indicate may be biased or questionable are re-reviewed by the ASWB examination committee. For a step-by-step guide to examination development, students are encouraged to visit the ASWB's website at http://www.aswb.org/SWLE/examdev.asp.

While there have been oral exams used in the past, they appear to have been pushed aside in favor of the easier-to-administer multiple-choice format. With the oral examinations, issues of validity and reliability would be present. However, the standardized multiple-choice format is problematic as well: an examination of barriers to licensure (Boutté-Queen, 2003) revealed that the "one correct response multiple choice format" may not adequately account for at least six different issues, including (1) differences in culture or ethnicity, (2) critical thinking and analysis, (3) test anxiety and preparation, (4) classroom versus practice knowledge, (5) clinical competencies, and, at the BSW level, (6) differences between the CSWE-required generalist practice perspective and the ASWB job analysis. Recent online discussions among MSW faculty indicate growing concern about the disconnection between CSWE's curricular requirements and the ASWB examination questions created by licensed practitioners. See also Thyer's call (2010) for more attention among social work educators to the rates at which graduates are passing the ASWB examinations and for a concerted effort to bring together or at least analytically discuss the two governing forces of the profession: CSWE's accreditation requirements and ASWB's examination content.

1. Differences in culture/ethnicity

ASWB submits its examinations to psychometric analysis as well as to expert scrutiny to minimize ethnic and gender bias; lately, more information on the statistical performance and bias of questions and answers has been made available (Marson et al., 2010). When a possibly biased item is identified through the statistical analysis, it is reviewed for content bias by ASWB's examination committee, which edits and reviews test questions and answers. The association works to ensure that the committee's composition is as expert and diverse as possible. Still, despite the ASWB's efforts to have cultural representation on the committee, 65 percent of the committee members in the past ten years have been white (see table 4.1). When a person of color or from a minority group leaves the committee, efforts to recruit another person of color or of a minority group are not always immediately successful. However, the work of the committee must continue. Therefore, the voices of minority groups may not always be fully represented, and at worst have the potential to be absent or merely a token presence with regard to test questions or appropriate responses.

In a recent update on the diversity of test item writers, the ASWB (2009a) asserts that diversity among those practitioners who submit examination questions and answers is improving. The intent is to develop the

TABLE 4.1 ASWB's TABLE OF EXAM COMMITTEE COMPOSITION, 1999–2009

YEAR (TOTAL NUMBERS)	NUMBER OF WHITE MEMBERS (% OF COMMITTEE)	NUMBER OF AFRICAN AMERICAN MEMBERS (% OF COMMITTEE)	NUMBER OF HISPANIC MEMBERS (% OF COMMITTEE)	ASIAN OR OTHER MEMBERS (% OF COMMITTEE)
1999 (14)	6 (43%)	4 (29%)	2 (14%)	2 (Asian) (14%)
2000 (14)	8 (57%)	5 (36%)	0	1 (Asian) (7%)
2001 (15)	8 (53%)	5 (33%)	2 (13%)	0
2002 (15)	11 (73%)	2 (13%)	2 (13%)	0
2003 (16)	12 (75%)	3 (19%)	1 (6%)	0
2004 (17)	11 (65%)	4 (23%)	1 (6%)	1 (Asian) (6%)
2005 (16)	7 (44%)	5 (30%)	2 (13%)	2 (1 Asian, 1 part Native American) (13%)
2006 (16)	11 (69%)	4 (25%)	1 (6%)	0
2007 (16)	13 (81%)	2 (13%)	0	1 (Asian) (6%)
2008 (18)	14 (78%)	3 (17%)	0	1 (Asian) (5%)
2009 (18)	14 (78%)	3 (17%)	0	1 (Asian) (5%)
Average 1999–2009	*65%*	*23%*	*6%*	*5%*

widest and most diverse pool of item writers possible on dimensions including areas of practice, years of experience, levels of education and training, geographic region, gender, and race and ethnicity. While the association's efforts in this regard are laudable, diversity in terms of total racial or ethnic and gender composition of the overall group of item writers continues to need attention. Most have been white. Boutté-Queen (2003) references Schriver (2001) when stating, "In intelligence testing, any advantage gained by test-takers of the same culture as those who created the tests is referred to as cultural bias" (Boutté-Queen, p. 40). Thus, while the authors of this text acknowledge that it is not necessary to be of a particular race or ethnicity to write or select appropriate question responses, having wide and diverse racial and ethnic representation on the committee would help reduce the cultural influence of individual item writers on the examination preparation process.

In addition to questions that could be raised about the racial or ethnic composition of item writers and selectors are questions relevant to the same characteristics of those who complete the job analysis, the results of which determine weights assigned to examination content areas. A review of the Social Work Job Analysis in Support of the American Association of State Social Work Board Examination Program (AASSWB, 1996), findings of which are used to determine the percentage weight given each content area of social work practice on licensing exams, indicates the majority of respondents to the 1995–96 job analysis were female and white. The "highest proportions of African American respondents were in the Basic (7.8 percent) and Advanced (7.7 percent) groups" (p. 12). Nationally, of the 3,808 respondents (23.4% of potential respondents), 3,111 self-identified as white, 226 as African American, 83 as Hispanic or Latino, 43 as Asian, and 22 as Native American (AASSWB, Appendix C, p. 2).

A more recent report on the scope of social work practice is available in the ASWB's (2004) *Analysis of the Practice of Social Work: 2003*. In each licensing category, the overwhelming majority of respondents were Caucasian or white. This group was followed most closely by African American or black, but the distance between groups was notable. Hispanic or Latino most often followed as a distant third. The most recent 2008 practice analysis has been completed just as this primer goes to press. ASWB's report is now available (ASWB, 2010b). Readers are encouraged to check out the racial and gender composition of respondents to this survey.

For some, racial- and ethnic-related barriers to success in taking a multiple-choice examination may include language differences. In an attempt to level the playing field for those for whom English is a second language, the ASWB has put forth a set of accommodations that include,

"two hours of extra time, a bilingual dictionary and/or an English dictionary, are allowed for ESL candidates whose jurisdictions grant approval."
The issue here, however, is that the individual jurisdictions must allow
these accommodations and not all do. Furthermore, despite the availability
of such allowances, there are still those for whom English is not the first
language who do not pass. The ASWB (2008b) acknowledges this when
reporting,

> For those with limited English, there is no way of determining whether fail-
> ure on the exams is due to language difficulties, cultural differences, or edu-
> cational experience. There has been very little research done to try to track
> down the major cause or causes: things that candidates seemed to be trying
> to explain on the survey with comments like "The dictionary was not help-
> ful; it did not have social work terminology," "some of the English words [I]
> cannot find in (bilingual) dictionary," or "I graduated with honors but I can-
> not seem to pass this exam." (p. 5)

2. CRITICAL THINKING AND ANALYSIS

In multiple-choice examinations, candidates must select the one correct
response, as if following the advice, "Don't think . . . don't analyze . . . just
read and choose." For some, it may appear that after years of being given
client-based scenarios and told to analyze each for the presence of a thor-
ough assessment, missing information, next step, and so on, the correct
response is based only on what the test question presents, not on what
the candidate has been trained to do given the complexities of practice.
Considering the interaction between people and their systems, the authors
find it troubling that those taking the test must choose the "best" response
among those listed at that moment, which may or may not be supported
by empirical evidence or applicable to all clients in a given situation.
Indeed, the literature (Johnson & Huff, 1987) indicates that such test formats may not actually measure what we refer to as social work knowledge
or even predict competence. To date, all but one state (California) requires
passing a multiple-choice examination to determine knowledge assessment
and practice competence. However, after approximately ten years of
administering a state-specific job analysis and testing method at a cost of
approximately $1 million per year, California's examination may soon be
changing (ASWB, 2008a).

Additional questions were raised by Randall and Thyer (1994), who
sought to determine whether the LCSW (clinical) exam was a valid instru-
ment. In their study, forty-two master's level students were given the fifty-
item advanced study guide that was sanctioned by ASWB at that time and

asked to select the correct answer. Prior to making the study guide available to participants, all the questions were blanked out so students were looking at only the multiple-choice response options. Based on the four-response options available one would surmise that students would have a one-in-four chance of selecting the correct response. However, the authors indicated that student responses were correct at a rate of 37 percent, not the expected rate of 25 percent, a statistically significant difference. These findings suggest that it was possible to guess the right answer more often than would be predicted if the guesses were based on chance, perhaps because of how the answers were phrased.

Thyer and Vodde (1994) report much the same findings in their effort to test the validity of the Academy of Certified Social Workers (ACSW) among a group of sixty-two master's level students. Again, this exam utilizes the four-choice, single-response format utilized with multiple-choice tests. This would lead one to believe that, based on a one-in-four chance of selecting the correct response, participants would choose the correct response approximately 25 percent of the time. One might even suggest that this number would be lower because the sample consisted of first-year students enrolled in a MSW program, and not of seasoned practitioners seeking certification at an advanced competence level. Using the same method of blanking out the questions and presenting only the four options from which to choose utilized by Randall and Thyer (1994), the researchers asked students to select the correct response. In this instance, students were correct approximately 41 percent of the time, which was not only statistically significant but also enough to question the validity of the ACSW examination at the time.

Furthermore, qualitative responses to Boutté-Queen's (2003) inquiry into barriers to successful licensure attainment indicate social work students may be ill prepared to take multiple-choice tests. One respondent indicated, "I feel frustrated with the licensure testing. After passing all of the classes and making good grades only to find I failed my BSW test" (p. 207), while another stated, "Referring to question #25 the textbook 'correct' answer assumes 1 size fits all and that's B.S." (p. 208). In an attempt to remedy this situation, one respondent indicated the examination should require an explanation from the examinee for selecting a response if that response was closely related to the correct response. Notably missing from this suggestion were the means (funding and personnel) by which these supplemental responses would be collected, reviewed, and graded. However, though we are now approximately fifteen to twenty years down the road, these calls still mirror that of Biggerstaff (1992), who called "for additional research designed to assess various test formats that would better measure skills to relevant practice, rather than using the current multiple-choice format, which does not allow for exploration of individual competence" (Boutté-Queen, 2003, p. 40).

3. TEST ANXIETY AND PREPARATION

The most competent of social workers can experience anxiety, fear, and possibly see fuzzy red lights and wandering pink elephants whenever multiple-choice test formats are presented. However, because this is the format that is used in most cases, the needs and learning styles of the applicant appear to be irrelevant at best. Middleman (1984) notes, "For any assessment process to discriminate reliably, the test takers need to be adequately and comparably prepared to show what they know. However, social workers are differentially prepared for standardized testing" (p. 151). In addition, after noting that some students are simply not prepared to take tests, Middleman indicates, "Research findings show test-taking 'smarts' in college students [are] more a function of an understanding and comprehension of tests and an ability to reason in test situations, than [they are] a function of knowledge of the subject matter" (p. 151). Moreover, the testing process itself, if it is experienced by students as similar to a motor vehicle exam (technical content, almost everybody passes, etc.), may result in dispiriting demoralization even when students pass it, a kind of discounting of the profession. This is in contrast to the experience of law students who, when they pass a rigorous bar exam are more proud of their profession, not less (personal communication, Dr. Tom Meenaghan, December 17, 2008).

Because of test anxiety or test-taking preparation inadequacies, in some instances the applicants fail and must test and retest until they pass the exam, despite having met all other criteria. No matter how high one's self-confidence is, even experienced and highly trained practitioners can have the breath knocked out of them when first receiving a failing examination score. In at least one state, the applicant must test and retest at least twice, each time failing within a certain number of points of passage, before they can request an alternative method of assessment. For example, in Texas, applicants who are unable to pass the ASWB examination are eligible to enroll in the Alternative Method of Examining Competency (AMEC) program, but only after they have failed the ASWB examination by not more than five points on two different occasions. In addition to costs paid during the initial testing process, the applicant must now submit $175 and an application to the Texas State Board of Social Work Examiners (2009) and be approved for entry.

On acceptance into the AMEC program, the applicant must be supervised weekly by a board-approved licensed social worker (often at an additional cost to the applicant if one is not available at the applicant's place of employment). The outcome is a portfolio chronicling the applicant's work toward licensure under the AMEC program, including documents describing the supervision process and papers providing insight into the applicant's knowledge of the practice of social work across a number of areas. This portfolio is then evaluated by an approved board evaluator. Outcomes may include the recommendation for granting of full licensure, provisionary licensure, or attainment of knowledge in certain content areas. This recommendation is reviewed by the full board, which then makes the final decision. While not perfect and certainly at additional cost(s) to the licensing applicant, this process offers a method by which licensure attainment can occur outside the multiple-choice, single-response format used across the country.

4. CLASSROOM VERSUS PRACTICE KNOWLEDGE

The question writers and item selectors must be licensed social workers. In some states, licensure comes only after a period of authorized supervised practice; as we have seen above, some states regulate only clinical practitioners. The *Analysis of the Practice of Social Work: 2003* (ASWB, 2004) indicates that of all U.S. respondents (n = 3,525), the greatest number of years in practice fell in the category of "at least 5 years but less than 10 years" (30 percent). This was followed by those who indicated they had been in practice "at least 3 years but less than 5" (18 percent). Just 6 percent of respondents indicated having been in practice twenty years or more. At least one respondent to Boutté-Queen's (2003) inquiry on barriers to licensure seems to have clearly noted a difference between practice and the questions asked on the licensing exam when stating, "The tests seem divorced from reality. Studying for the test wasn't about social work, just about passing the test and study courses are presented that way. Where do they get those questions anyhow?" (p. 208).

5. CLINICAL COMPETENCIES

The presence of licensed practitioners on the examination committee and the job analysis that obtains feedback from social workers employed in a variety of settings (often related to mental health), perhaps with a number of years of experience, increase the potential for clinically oriented questions on the basic bachelor's-level exam. Unfortunately, discourse over clinical versus other forms of practice is not new, as is noted in the literature. For example, while acknowledging the efforts of NASW toward ensuring a balance between the private practice or clinical side of practice and the broader aspects of social work states, Garcia (1990b) observes,

> In terms of a broader social agenda for the profession, there are a number of social workers who believe that it is appropriate and necessary for the professional association to be concerned about major societal issues such as the AIDS crisis, homelessness, poverty, substance abuse, racism, sexism, and homophobia and to support policy to address these social problems. The responsibilities of the profession must go beyond those which are self-serving. Interest and commitment to these broad social issues is not "antiprofessionalism." (p. 506)

Though this statement was made nearly twenty years ago, the perspectives of those required to take the licensing examination still reflect concerns about the clinical nature of the exam itself. Qualitative feedback presented in Boutté-Queen (2003) includes the following from test takers: "The LMSW exam relies too much on the mental health aspect of practice, not all LMSW's work in a mental health setting" (p. 208); other feedback states that the exam was a useful tool, however, "I also believe that if we keep the exam model, it should cover more areas of SW practice. It currently has a clinical focus" (p. 208).

6. DIFFERENCES BETWEEN THE CSWE-REQUIRED GENERALIST PRACTICE PERSPECTIVE AND THE ASWB JOB ANALYSIS

The CSWE requires that "the explicit curriculum at the BSW level [and MSW foundation] is designed to prepare graduates for generalist practice through mastery of the core competencies" (2008, p. 3). Descriptions and definitions of generalist practice change from program to program and are not necessarily guided by the national job analysis conducted by the ASWB, however. At minimum, this leaves the potential for gaps between what is being sanctioned as generalist practice by CSWE, what is being taught in classrooms across the country to BSW and MSW level students, and content for which ASWB is testing in terms of knowledge or competence. This is, perhaps, where BSW and MSW licensees find the most incongruence between their education and the testing process, and the same also may be true of MSW licensees who experience differences between what they learned in the classroom and the knowledge for which they are responsible at the time they take the examination. It also raises the question of whether the CSWE 2008 educational policy and accreditation standards, which focus on measurement of competencies as determinants of student outcomes, are moving in the direction of the ASWB examinations, which seek to measure competencies via the standardized, multiple-choice testing method. While improvements over the years have been made in the ASWB examinations, challenges remain. License applicants are encouraged to contact ASWB and their local board to take advantage of the information now available on the development of the examination and support in preparation for taking it. An additional consideration is whether the use of practitioners to develop test questions might lend itself to the proliferation of current practice fads being represented in the test question bank as opposed to evidence-based, tried-and-true methods. However, given ASWB's record of item-writer training, the rigorous process of review and approval of test items, the use of item writers from across the country, and the actual testing of items prior to use as a scored question, it is apparent that efforts are made to preclude this from occurring.

Exemptions: Destination Deferred?

After reviewing the development of legal regulation of social work practice in the United States, Barker and Branson (2000) conclude, "Licensure for social workers in all jurisdictions has been a difficult journey which has yet to be completed" (p. 193). Even now that each state has in place some form of regulation of social work, in many states there are so many regulations and so many broad exemptions that clients who use social work services may not benefit from the protections that licensure is intended to provide. This gap in protection and regulation has developed because in most jurisdictions political compromises were required to pass initial licensing legislation. A grandparenting or blanketing-in period, usually limited to one or two years after licensing begins, has been typically available for candidates to apply for licensure without having to meet the testing and other eligibility requirements. About half of the jursisdictions turned to a grandparenting strategy when licensure was first established (Bibus, 2007, citing a Cloutier's 1997 master's thesis survey of NASW chapters). Thus, the pool of licensed social workers in many states often includes some who do not have accredited social work degrees and have not taken and passed the ASWB examination.

In addition, in most states there are exempted categories of social workers who are not required to be licensed. Frequently, in addition to the customary exemption for students in their field practicum placements, these categories include social workers employed by federal, state, county, or municipal government agencies or schools. Only five states have no exemptions (though seven more list no exemptions except for qualified other professionals; see Table 1: Board Structure/Statutory Provisions at www.aswb.org). Notably, however, states such as North Carolina and Alabama have eliminated earlier enacted exemptions for public sector social workers; for instance, a recent comprehensive reform of Alabama's child welfare system required all child welfare workers "to obtain licensure within one year of employment (Walley, 2007, p. 19).

ASWB's commentary on its model act points out that "there are no exemptions to social work practice in the Model Act, except for students currently participating in an approved social work program, when completing an internship or externship, or other social work experience required for such programs" (p. 4). However, there is recognition that bringing every social worker's practice under regulatory provisions in every state so that everyone who uses social work services, social work professionals, and the public have access to the protections that licensing provides is an ideal that political realities make difficult to achieve. So boards aspiring to the ideal are encouraged to limit exemptions as much as possible and to keep grandparenting policies narrow and brief. As it is, in many states confusion easily arises as to the educational background and competencies of licensed social workers when a service user cannot tell if the licensee was licensed under grandparenting and thus may not have a social work degree and may not have taken an examination establishing minimum competencies. Just as egregiously, people who use the services of unlicensed social workers who fall under exemptions in their state may not realize that their social worker may fail to meet minimum qualifications required by law of licensees, and will not have recourse to make a complaint to the local board of social work if services are below standards.

Although some exemptions do not appear to diminish public safety—such as those for practitioners from other disciplines like psychology or nursing who engage in activities that are similar to social workers' practice behaviors (e.g., counseling or case management) and who carry their own professional licenses—exempting social workers practicing in public social service settings does raise public protection concerns. This type of exemption erodes public confidence and fosters confusion among the public and the media as to who is and who is not a social worker (NASW, 2005). The exemption also may contribute negatively to the image of public social services. "Exemptions in licensing laws for practitioners employed by local, state and federal government sponsored agencies may create the perception by consumers of a 'second-class' service-delivery system within the public agencies" (Thyer & Biggerstaff, 1989, p. 23). Yet empirical studies have yet to establish that either grandparented or exempt social workers' practice is more or less effective than the practice of licensed colleagues with degrees in social work (Pardeck et al., 1997).

A strategy that some states have adopted that is intended to shore up this subversion of the purpose of licensing short of requiring licensure for public government social workers is instituting in-service training for social workers in public agencies that is similar in content to social work education. Cohen and Deri (1992, p. 157) and other social work educators endorse this continuing education strategy as potentially reducing "the possibility of a two-class service delivery system emerging in states where a large number of social workers have been licensed through grandparenting" or are exempt from licensing altogether. Public funding for agency employees to pursue a social work degree, such as use of Social Security Title IV-E funds to subsidize the education of child welfare practitioners who will be working with families and children who are poor, also appears to be a promising strategy. Recruitment efforts may be fostered, thereby increasing the number of educated social work service providers. However, this does not necessarily translate into an increase in the number or proportion of licensed social workers.

Unless exemptions are repealed, clients who believe their social worker's practice has fallen below standards do not have access to licensing boards and must rely instead on either intra-agency grievance processes (which tend to focus on eligibility appeals and not on practitioner competence) or expensive civil law suits. Although the process for investigating and responding to complaints administered by licensing boards is imperfect and subject to criticism for being too lenient (with a great majority of complaints being dismissed) or too invasive (with investigators using adversarial tactics or withholding information from the social workers who are the subjects of complaints), it is a "third-party" process that is separate from the employing agency's potential conflicts of interest, and available at no cost and in a less-intimidating manner to any client or member of the public.

So, why do some social workers oppose mandatory licensing of all social workers, including those employed in public agencies. Reasons provided over the years in one state (Minnesota; Bibus, 2007; Holcomb, 2003) include

1. the cost to employees having to pay licensing fees may possibly then be passed on to government budgets (and thus taxpayers) as part of labor agreements,
2. smaller rural public agencies might face recruitment and hiring shortages because fewer applicants would have the credentials required,
3. licensing is not needed for public protection because public

elected officials are ultimately in charge of government services
and provide oversight and accountability,

4. there is a satisfactory process already in place for handling complaints or grievances by clients, and

5. the layers of supervision within public agency social services
already ensure competency and standards.

As summarized by the coordinator of the coalition of licensed social
workers who surveyed the opinions of county social workers in Minnesota
(Luinenburg, 2005), one objection to removing the exemption is at a systemic level: licensure represents an intrusion and interference, unnecessary regulation, and accompanying costs. The complaint process could
damage the reputation of the agency. The complaint process needs to be
improved and become less adversarial, with more use of mediation. A second set of objections arises at the individual worker level: some staff who
have applied voluntarily for licensure feel that they have been treated
unfairly, for example in not being approved for a clinical license. Some
resent the implication that if they do not have BSW or MSW degrees they
are not good social workers. Some agency directors urge those employees
who have voluntarily become licensed to drop their licenses due to the
intrusive and distracting nature of complaint investigations. Third, licensure is seen as divisive, setting up a hierarchy that threatens the multidisciplinary team. Because social workers share so many functions with other
disciplines, this is an issue for licensed social workers more than for other
licensed professions in the public sector such as licensed public health
nurses. (See box 4.1 for sample quotations from two public agency social
workers.)

In fact, many public social service directors in Minnesota believe that
the costs for agencies to cover employees' licensing fees or for employees
to pay the fees themselves, particularly during periods of economic
downturns and budget cuts when their wages are being frozen, would be
a considerable burden. New licensees would, they believe, need to obtain
more supervision than is required by agencies, and additional employees
with credentials necessary for licensing supervision may need to be
hired. Finally, the directors tend to agree with the second objection noted
above: the pool of potential applicants for social work positions would
be limited to licensees only; this is potentially a particular hardship for
rural agencies that are already struggling to fill vacancies with qualified
applicants and for applicants of color. "The labor market is simply not as
broad in rural communities. In addition, considering barriers people of
color may face in achieving advanced degrees, [repealing exemptions]

could negatively impact the ability of counties to recruit and retain staff of color" (Minnesota Association of County Social Service Administrators, 2003).

Nevertheless, social workers in public agencies provide vital services to people who are in the most vulnerable circumstances. The city, county, or state agency is often the refuge of last resort for people lacking basic needs, individuals who are in danger of abuse or neglect and desperate for protection, families seeking support in caring for loved ones or under pressure to apply for public assistance, persons suffering from illness and without insurance coverage or access to competent treatment and case management, people who have a right to public social services for developmental or age-related conditions, and the children and adults for whom the public social service agency is ultimately responsible. In other words, potentially all of us at some point in our lives will use the services of our local agency social worker. Public agency social workers maintain the infrastructure of social supports, health care, corrections, income maintenance, job training, housing stability, community resources, neighborhood viability, service development and coordination, child welfare, family services, and human rights advocacy.

Many clients referred for public social services are involuntary, which sets up adversarial dynamics, at least at first (Daley & Doughty, 2007; Rooney, 2009). To transcend these potentially harmful interactions requires patient, persistent, careful, informed, and sophisticated social work competencies. If social workers practice ethically, then renewed hope, effective help, and success in achieving goals are likely outcomes. In the rare circumstances when a social worker's practice does not meet minimum standards, clients deserve an opportunity for redress beyond what might be available within the county or state social service system itself. For licensed social workers, the standards and procedures established through licensing can play a role in sustaining and nurturing as well as regulating their good practice.

Therefore, boards of social work are working diligently to modify existing exemptions and, if that is not possible, to encourage voluntary licensing. Studies such as Boutté-Queen's (2003) provide guidance to what licensees might perceive as barriers to maintaining their licenses. Cost is one factor, but so are these: the knowledge that a license is not required for the job, the difficulties in obtaining supervision, the fear of destabilizing a collegial and multidisciplinary team, the lack of plans to move to a nonexempt setting, and the perception that the process of investigating complaints is unfair or unduly arduous (Sheryl McNair, LICSW, assistant director, Minnesota Board of Social Work, personal communication, September 21, 2007). Efforts to educate licensees and administrators as well as the public and educators about the purpose and benefits of licensure could be most fruitful: "Most important appears to be the need to educate those who administer agencies and organizations that hire social workers since the personal need of license seekers [to be licensed] appears to be related to employment status" (Boutté-Queen, 2003, p. 148).

Another reason to pursue repeal of exemptions is the importance of supervision for competent (and licensed) social work practice. Comparing the experience with supervision of social workers who were licensed against the experience with supervision of social workers who were not licensed, Gray (1990) finds that "supervision under licensure conditions was significantly more likely to be held for longer periods of time . . . , [and] licensure was associated with frequent, weekly supervision" (p. 58). Regular and frequent sessions between supervisor and supervisee are among the primary factors related to effective supervision (Bibus, 1993; Bogo & McKnight, 2005). Licensed supervisors also are required for tapping medical assistance and insurance reimbursement, a critical asset during these times of budget shortfalls.

One of the objections often raised to licensing or to repealing exemptions is that there is little evidence to show that licensed social workers practice more effectively than nonlicensed social workers. Thus far, no studies have explored clients' perspectives regarding the quality of services from licensed social workers compared to services from unlicensed social workers. Such studies would be difficult and costly to design and conduct, but, given that the fundamental purpose of licensure is to set minimum professional practice standards and provide protection for clients when those standards are not met, investment in this research seems worthwhile. There is a chance that statistically significant differences between licensed and unlicensed social work practice might not be detected (e.g., Pardeck et al., 1997); even if such were the case, though, access to an independent board to redress harm resulting from incompetent or unethical practice is a valuable legal right in itself. This legal right should be present no matter which social worker a client happens to be assigned to. And more information about factors that lead to helpful and ethical practices would result from more study.

Another barrier to licensing in public service settings is the perception on the part of unions that their members might not be well served by a licensing requirement. However, it is possible that union members would see an exemption from licensing in some situations as a liability and perceive licensing as an asset. "An alternative union strategy would be to not insist on exemption, but, instead, to demand that public welfare personnel receive the necessary training to qualify for licensure" (Karger, 1988, p. 44). Also important to consider are Pardeck and colleagues' (1997) recommendations for innovative strategies in regulating social work practice: to counteract potential exclusion of minorities (who might not have had access to social work education), they suggest that boards consider a process of certification that credits practice experience under supervision for eligibility to take competency examinations that would include case examples as well as standard multiple-choice formats. It will be important to involve all constituents in developing a proposal that would modify the exemption for public social workers by requiring that practitioners with accredited social work degrees be licensed. "There are ways to legally regulate all social workers without exemptions and fill social service and child welfare positions with them" (DeAngelis, 2001, p. 11; see also NASW, 2005).

BOX 4.1 VOICES OF PUBLIC AGENCY SOCIAL WORKERS: TWO EXAMPLES FROM OVERSON, 2005

I also feel that many people employed in the county system have received their excellent social work skills from years of experience, not a license. . . . If licensing was a requirement, clients would be in jeopardy of losing quality social workers that have been a crucial part of their treatment teams. (Quoted in Overson, p. 49)

I feel social workers should be licensed for the same reasons that nurses are licensed. Workers with unrelated degrees and experiences are often hired as social workers and a requirement to be licensed would ensure some quality control in the workplace. (Quoted in Overson, p. 58)

Faculty Licensure: A Special Case?

One of the most contentious issues dividing social work educators is whether or not those who teach social work should have a license to practice social work (see box 4.2). Some states do consider teaching social work as social work practice and their state law therefore regulates faculty members who are social workers (e.g., Alabama, Georgia, Hawaii, Maine, and Minnesota); a few require only faculty members who teach direct practice or field to be licensed. In most states, social work faculty are exempt from licensing at this time, but, as noted above, ASWB's Model Social Work

Practice Act recommends against such exemptions. In response to ASWB's model act, which also specifies that social work practice includes education and teaching social work, the National Association of Deans and Directors of Social Work Programs (NADD) and the CSWE took official positions opposing mandatory licensing of social work faculty (CSWE, 2001). The position statement issued by the CSWE

> recognizes and supports the importance of licensing as a mechanism for the protection of the public where social workers have a direct relationship with clients or patients. . . . [However,] there is no evidence that licensing of educators is necessary to protect the public. (p. 8)

Concerns were expressed regarding development of varying standards from state to state that would threaten the integrity of national accreditation, disrupt faculty mobility, and increase barriers to recruitment of diverse faculty. In the view of CSWE and NADD, traditional administrative systems in higher education of accreditation, peer review, and academic protocols are sufficient for public protection from social work professors whose practice falls below standards. (See ASWB, 2002; and Matz, 1996.)

When faculty licensure is raised on the list services that social work educators use to discuss issues, responses tend to come in immediately, copiously, and vigorously. In preparation for participating in a panel hosted by ASWB in spring, 2002, Spencer Zeiger, the Association of Baccalaureate Social Work Program Directors (BPD) president at the time, reported that a BPD electronic mailing list discussion on licensing of faculty reflected 27 percent of posted responses in favor of licensure for social work educators, 3 percent in favor of recommending (not requiring) licensure, 8 percent in favor of limited licensing (e.g., for those teaching direct practice or field), and 62 percent opposed to licensure for social work educators.

> "This was the hottest topic that I've ever seen on the listserv [sic]," [Zeiger] said. . . . In addition to criticisms voiced by Leashore and Beless [two other panelists] regarding licensure's inability to guarantee effective teaching abilities and academia's built-in quality controls, Zeiger said that those opposed to licensing also cited issues including time and expense, restricted mobility, and questions about the applicability of licensing examination items and the knowledge areas of faculty members. (ASWB, 2002, p. 4)

Another common objection to licensing social work educators (often the first voiced) is that students are not clients; critics point to serious ethical challenges such as clarification of boundaries and purpose if students are considered to be clients. Some who favor licensing of faculty counter that students use the services of their professors and are in this way in fact clients and quite vulnerable, too, due to the power differential between faculty and students and the poor record that academic institutions have in disciplining faculty members who have exploited students for their own gain. Others in favor of licensing faculty agree with opponents that the purpose and meaning of students' relationships with faculty are distinct from the purpose and meaning of clients' work with social workers, but they favor licensing for other reasons. For example, other panelists at the ASWB conference in 2002 (social work professors Carlton Munson, Tony Bibus, and Gail Johnson) argue, "Faculty [status] is supposed to be the pinnacle of the profession, Munson said, and should always demonstrate the highest professional standards. 'If faculty are not licensed, students will want to know why.'" (ASWB, 2002, p. 4)

Arguments for and against social work educators being licensed social workers tend to elaborate on points raised in a published debate between Thyer (2000) and Seidl (2000) regarding whether social work faculty members who teach clinical practice should have a clinical social work license. Claims that licensing is intended to foster high standards of practice and provide an independent recourse for clients when social work services fall short of minimum standards are met with demands to produce evidence that licensing improves practice or indeed protects vulnerable clients. As we have reviewed in chapter 1, such evidence is minimal, but no other profession's licensure is empirically based, and some professors from other professional disciplines (such as law and medicine) are licensed, and, when asked about it, do not understand why this would be controversial for social work colleagues.

Still, pragmatic concerns as well as those based on ethical principles are raised in opposition to licensing faculty members.

- Requiring licensing would severely limit the already-too-shallow pool of prospective candidates for the increasing number of social work faculty vacancies in the United States, curtailing efforts to expand the diversity of the professoriate.
- Many current faculty members may not qualify for licensure in their states (e.g., they are generalist social workers not specializing in clinical practice in a state that only licenses clinicians; Seidl calls the plethora of various idiosyncratic regulations across the states a "many splendored thing" [2000, p. 194]).
- Licensing policies and requirements may discriminate against some groups of faculty (for example, in Minnesota faculty teaching

in private colleges and universities might be required to be licensed while colleagues in public institutions are exempt).

· Fees and other costs of licensing could be burdensome for some.

· Simply being licensed might lead to the presumption that any licensed social worker should be able to assume a faculty position regardless of the scholarship, leadership, teaching competencies, or other qualifications usually required for tenure.

· Academic freedom could be jeopardized with licensed faculty constrained by state regulations or by the need to focus narrowly on direct practice to the detriment of critical analysis of social policy or advocacy for social justice and human rights.

Teaching is not practice, many faculty members believe; many deans and directors agree with Seidl that deciding who teaches social work "is an academic decision and not a professional one" (2000, p. 196).

Conversely, Thyer (2000) favors modifying accreditation standards to require licensing for faculty who teach direct practice. Such a standard would enhance social work education by raising the credibility faculty would gain by submitting to licensure. Licensing requires licensees to keep updated with continuing education and supervision as well as to have undergone a criminal background check, for example. "There are added elements of being subject to the state's social work code of ethics and mechanisms for responding to complaints and grievances" (p. 200).

A recent exchange between the editor and a reader of the *Journal of Social Work Values and Ethics* (Liles, 2008) demonstrates that the debate continues. Editor Marson (2006) asks, "How could a profession even consider the option of not having a license" when other professional faculty do? Reader Liles replies, "Simply requiring practice faculty to have a license or obtain a license will not guarantee competence in matters related to practice, although it might be a good beginning standard." Box 4.2 summarizes some of the positions held by supporters and opponents of faculty licensure.

Perhaps in all this back and forth, Prof. Harriet Scott's commentary (e-mail posting on the BPD List, 3/28/02) is the wisest:

As soon as we start splitting hairs about who are social workers who need to be licensed and who do not need to be licensed, we are opening the doors to eliminating licensing rather than trying to ask the state to administer a complex differentiation of who social workers are. We need to spend our energies interpreting to the public and legislators what social work is, not trying

Box 4.2. Sample Positions For and Against Licensing Social Workers Who Teach Social Work

For:

- Ethical principles, such as providing instruction only in areas in which one has established competence, are incorporated in licensing statutes and rules.
- It is important that instructors be legally sanctioned to practice in the area they teach.
- Licensed professors are held accountable to standards of conduct, continuing education and supervision requirements, and so on, and their credibility is thus enhanced.
- Much of teaching is modeling good practice: licensed professors model the value of maintaining a professional license as a social worker.
- Licensing increases public trust, political power, recognition with other licensed professions, market share, and potential for vendorship.
- Submitting to the jurisdiction of licensing boards affirms social work educators' accountability and the importance of government regulation in social work education under constitutional delegation of powers.

Against:

- There is no evidence that requiring social work educators to be licensed would increase public protection or improve teaching and learning outcomes.
- Licensing often places undue emphasis on direct micropractice without recognizing the integral role of macropractice, community development and organization, research, or policy practice in social work.
- Teaching is not the same as practice.
- Requiring licensing for faculty positions would shrink and homogenize the pool of candidates, which is already too small and lacks diversity.
- Licensing threatens academic freedom, and restricts independence of inquiry, free generation of ideas, principled hiring decisions, and open challenges to the status quo.
- If a professor is not practicing outside the classroom, there is no need to maintain a license to practice.

to convince them that social work educators are not social workers in need of licensing.

The Relationship Between Licensing and Association Membership: Forced Choice?

Despite the role of the professional associations in promoting licensure, licensing may present a serious threat to the sustainability of the associations themselves. For example, in some states social workers are choosing to maintain their licenses while dropping their membership in NASW. Results of a recent e-mailed survey of NASW members in Texas provide some information regarding the perceived benefits of professional association membership. The survey was sent to approximately 5,000 members who are engaged with the Texas chapter through a chapter LISTSERV. Of the 5,000 members, 1,005 responded, for a response rate of approximately 20 percent. Given that the survey was mailed once a week over a three-week data-collection period, this response is acceptable, although it is not generalizable to the entire body of NASW Texas members or NASW as a whole. Still, useful information was obtained (figure 4.2). For example, most of the respondents were licensed, and one fourth were working in not-for-profit organizations (n = 235; 27%). More than two thirds (n = 599; 69.4%) indicated their employment setting required them to be licensed; the largest number of respondents were licensed at the master's level without clinical specialty (n = 355; 43.7%), with the respondent paying related licensing fees (n = 746; 88%) at a higher rate than did employers (n = 80; 9%) or a combination of employer and self (n = 23; 2.7%).

Respondents also indicated that the most helpful benefit of professional associations were professional newsletters (n = 903) and journal subscriptions (n = 901). Additional benefits are seen in figure 4.3.

Opportunities most often cited as being beneficial to respondents include continuing education units (n = 899) and professional networking (n = 894). A total picture of opportunities and how often they are deemed beneficial is seen in figure 4.4.

One perhaps unintentional result of the efforts to regulate social work practice is the significant difference in numbers of licensed social workers and NASW members. Nationally, as of this writing NASW boasts 150,000 members in fifty-six chapters (www.socialworkers.org). However, there are far more licensed social workers than there are NASW members in many states. For example, in 2003 there were approximately 5,600 NASW members in the state of Texas, but licensing data indicated there were more than 15,000 licensed social workers in the same state. As of September

Figure 4.2 Who Pays License Fee?

Who pays the cost of your licensure?

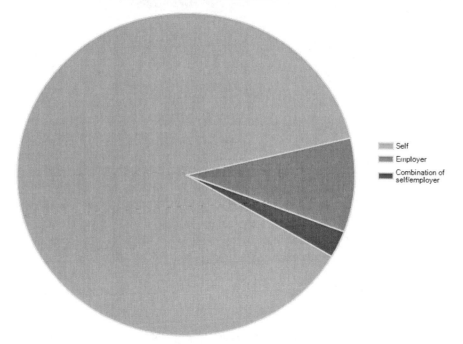

Self
Employer
Combination of self/employer

2009, NASW Texas chapter showed a membership of 5,600 (roughly the same as 2003 figures) and ASWB indicated there were 20,621 licensed social workers (a gain of approximately 5,600). Table 4.2 shows summer 2009 figures in terms of NASW membership and licensed social workers in the nine states with the largest NASW membership rosters. In seven states, there are significant differences with NASW membership far lower than the number of licensees in the state:

As Boutté-Queen (2003) indicates, choices between licensure attainment and professional association membership may often leave professional organizations at a loss of membership because individuals must make financial choices. Though not statistically significant, quantitative responses indicate costs are more likely to be cited as barriers to licensure attainment for members of minority groups. Qualitative comments ranged from those who indicated financial costs were part of any profession and therefore not a problem, to

Cost is the biggest barrier. I am applying for Arkansas licensure and had to pay a $200 application fee, $45 for criminal history checks, and will have to

FIGURE 4.3 BENEFITS OF PROFESSIONAL ASSOCIATION MEMBERSHIP

The following benefits associated with professional social work association memberships are useful to me as they relate to my professional practice:

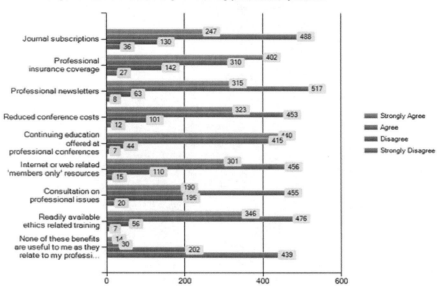

Source: Authors.

pay an additional $200 when I take the test. I think this is outrageous! (Quoted in Boutté-Queen, 2003, p. 119)

Indeed, in the 2009 survey of NASW members in Texas, Boutté-Queen (2009) found that approximately 16 percent (n = 145) of respondents had at some point in time not renewed their professional association membership in order to obtain or renew their professional license. Of this number, 70 percent indicated the professional association membership that was not renewed was membership in NASW. At the time of the survey, 12 percent (n = 108) indicated they were not members of a professional association because the cost of membership conflicted with licensure obtainment or renewal. We will return to the importance of professional associations and their role in our practice as distinguished from licensing in the next chapter. Of particular concern related to affording membership as a current and future issue is the recently adopted increase in fees for the examination (ASWB, 2009c), especially in the current recession and in the context of the debt load for many graduates of social work programs.

Emerging Issues: What Is on the Horizon?

Each of the controversial areas addressed in this chapter is likely to remain at issue for some years to come. As they have in the past, debate

FIGURE 4.4 OPPORTUNITIES MADE POSSIBLE THROUGH ASSOCIATION MEMBERSHIP

The following opportunities, as they are made possible through professional association memberships, is useful to me:

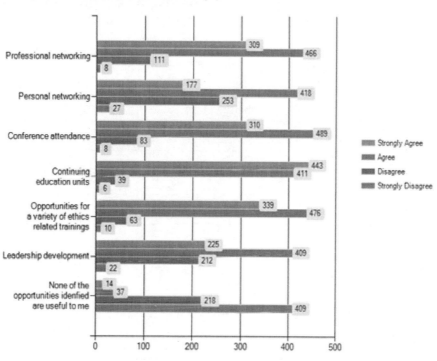

Source: Authors.

and questions will continue regarding the purpose of social work regulation, the definition of practice, the scope of licensed practice, the use of standardized examinations to measure competence, alternative paths to licensure, exemptions, fees for licensing jeopardizing membership in professional associations, and, as we will see in the next section, the need for more substantial research to justify regulatory policies. In addition, several other key issues have been emerging lately that may presage debates and controversies on the horizon that licensed social workers and regulators may increasingly face. Here we highlight four of these "hot topics."

First, the growth of electronic, communication, and information technology (e.g., e-mail, cell phones, copying and scanning machines, faxes, Internet chats and blogs, text messages, webcams, interactive TV, and so on) has opened a frontier of practice and with it new challenges. Second, this frontier reveals new questions involving even established features of licensure, such as supervision. Third, the relationship between and

TABLE 4.2 CONTRAST BETWEEN NUMBER OF NASW MEMBERS AND NUMBER OF LICENSEES

STATE	RANGE OF NASW MEMBERSHIP	NUMBER OF LICENSED SOCIAL WORKERS*	DIFFERENCE BETWEEN NASW MEMBERSHIP AND NUMBER OF LICENSED SOCIAL WORKERS REPORTED
New York	10,000+ members	49,469	39,469
California	10,000+ members	21,688	11,688
Texas	5,000–10,000	20,621	10,621
Florida	5,000–10,000	9,645	(55) at highest NASW point
Illinois	5,000–10,000	12,130	2,130
Massachusetts	5,000–10,000	21,633	11,633
Michigan	5,000–10,000	27,378	17,378
New Jersey	5,000–10,000	16,461	6,461
Pennsylvania	5,000–10,000	10,718	718

* Provided by Troy Elliott, ASWB communications director, September 28, 2009.

distinctions among helping professions are ever evolving: some are historically regulated, some are recently regulated, and some are not yet regulated. Some professions may be laying claim to expertise formerly held nearly exclusively by social work and may even threaten to displace social work. For instance, the perception among hospital administrators that nurses can provide case management services and discharge planning has resulted in the elimination of social work positions in some health centers. Fourth, recent disasters have brought to the forefront the need for special or relaxed regulations to govern emergency responses. As with issues discussed earlier in this chapter, these emerging issues interrelate dynamically.

Cyber Practice

"Nurse Involved in Suicide Chats Loses License." This is the headline to a recent newspaper article reporting an action taken by the Minnesota

Board of Nursing against a licensee who had participated in online discussions posing as an expert in suicide techniques (Walsh, 2009, p. A1). Two other participants in the same Internet chat room did commit suicide. The board found that this nurse had

> engaged in unethical conduct, including but not limited to, conduct likely to deceive, defraud, or harm the public, by using false identities, encouraging individuals to commit suicide via the Internet, watching individuals commit suicide with a webcam, and telling individuals that his nursing experience gave him "expert knowledge into the most effective ways to kill yourself." (Minnesota Board of Nursing, 2009, p. 3)

For this infraction and many other earlier practice deficiencies for which the board had previously disciplined the licensee, the board revoked the nurse's license. This case illustrates the need for protective regulation of all forms of practice and delivery of services, not just of services delivered in person. (Interestingly, it also illustrates the importance of regulation as complementary to criminal proceedings, which in this case have only just now begun, after the board's action.)

In 2005, NASW and ASWB jointly published a set of standards to guide social workers in use of online as well as other communication and information technologies. Existing standards, rules, and statutes had presumed that most contact between practitioners and clients would be in person and in a specific locale and hence easily identifiable venue. Both licensing boards and licensees had been experiencing the limitations of this presumption, given the increasing use and availability of virtual practice modalities that did not involve in-person contact and that could be initiated from anywhere in the world and offered to anyone in the board's venue. Jurisdiction issues arose immediately. If a social worker living in one state is providing services to clients who live in other states across the country, which regulatory body or bodies have jurisdiction? Where is the venue of practice: in the state where the social worker lives and presumably is licensed or in the state where the client lives? Must licensees become licensed in every state where potential clients might access an Internet connection for social work or tele-mental-health services provided by the licensee?

As we have seen with earlier issues, a uniform nationwide strategy to address such questions is desirous but not typically developed in the United States. Many states use the client's residence as the governing factor and require social workers who are providing online services to residents in the state to be licensed by that state. In Minnesota, for example, a social worker in any other jurisdiction would have to obtain a social work license from the Minnesota Board of Social Work before offering tele-counseling services to any client in Minnesota. Other states require only that social workers providing online services in their states submit to regulation (i.e., licensing requirements) in the social worker's state of residence. Some states require that social workers be licensed both in the state of their residence and in that of their clients. Finally, some states' regulations do not yet address electronic practice across state lines.

The NASW/ASWB standards guide (NASW/ASWB, 2005) was developed because use of technology as an exclusive mode of practice as well as adjunctive tool for traditional in-person practice is increasing in prevalence and complexity. Referring to this increase as "an immense expansion" (p. 6), the document states four goals of the standards: to maintain and improve the quality of services, to guide social workers in incorporating technology in their practice, to help them monitor and evaluate use of technology, and to inform clients and regulatory bodies (among others) about professional standards in the use of technology (p. 4). Critical issues covered in the standards include the blurring of jurisdiction for regulation "when state lines and national boundaries are crossed electronically" (NASW/ASWB, 2005, p. 6). There are ten standards related to the following:

1. Ethics and Values,
2. Access,
3. Cultural Competence and Vulnerable Populations,
4. Technical Competencies,
5. Regulatory Competencies,
6. Identification and Verification,
7. Privacy/Confidentiality/Documentation/Security,
8. Risk Management,
9. Practice Competencies (of which there are six elaborated), and
10. Continuing Education.

Under the Regulatory Competencies standard (NASW/ASWB, 2005, p. 11), we find

> Social workers should understand that in some jurisdictions, the delivery of social work services is deemed to take place at the location of the client. It is the social worker's responsibility to contact the regulatory board(s) [to notify the board] of intent to provide services and find out what requirements are necessary to provide services legally in those jurisdictions.

The main point for students and licensees is to be sure to check with their own boards and the states where potential clients live before delivering services. Using technology competently to better inform and serve clients as well as to advocate for clients and for improved services is required for ethical and effective practice today—and so is planning for other actions and for contingencies when technologies fail.

With the federal government moving toward requiring more-transparent communication among health-care providers and expanding the sharing of medical records, new threats to privacy, self-determination, and informed consent may arise.

> State boards can anticipate that state and federal legislatures and agencies will be involved in efforts to streamline the flow of health information and that these efforts may involve changes in traditional arenas of state regulatory power, in areas such as confidentiality and privilege for mental health records. (NASW, 2007)

Interpretive guidelines in NASW/ASWB standards advise licensees again and again to follow applicable laws and rules. For example, "Supervision for purposes of licensure is governed by regulatory boards that may have specific definitions and requirements pertaining to the use of technology in supervision" (2005, p. 20). As yet unforeseen challenges are likely to emerge related to the use of technology, so keeping in touch with the board of social work is key to addressing this emerging issue.

Supervision

In most states, social work regulations require applicants for licensure or initially licensed practitioners to be supervised by licensed social workers and to submit documentation that those requirements have been met before they are allowed to practice independently. Supervision of practice has long been an essential part of social work, and social work scholars have historically led the way in development of theoretical models of supervision as well as research on effectiveness of supervision (e.g., Bogo & McKnight, 2005; Bruce & Austin, 2000; Bunker & Wijnberg, 1988; Caspi & Reid, 2002; Kadushin & Harkness, 2002; Kaiser, 1997; Munson, 2002; Poertner, 2006; Shulman, 1993, 2008; Tsui, 2005). "Supervision of students and practitioners has been central to social work since its earliest evolution as a recognized profession" (Shulman, 2008, p. 186). There are indications that licensure can lead to supervision in social work that is more structured (Gray, 1990).

Most often, regulators conceptualizing supervisory practices have pre-ferred in-person and one-to-one contact between supervisor and super-visee. For example, in Minnesota half the required supervision hours must be through one-to-one in-person contact between supervisor and super-visee (and not in a group supervision setting). Indeed, in a recent national analysis of supervisory knowledge, skills, and attitudes, supervisors rated monitoring use of technology with supervisees the lowest in importance, frequency, and criticality among competencies in the category of work context (ASWB, 2009b, p. E4). Nevertheless, use of emerging technologies is likely to rise in importance and frequency for licensing supervisors and to become critical to addressing the shortage of qualified supervisors experienced in many sectors.

Meanwhile, because regulating boards consider supervision a mainstay for ensuring competent and ethical practice and often use enhanced super-vision as part of disciplinary orders when licensees' practice falls below standards, requirements imposed on both supervisors and supervisees have grown in number and complexity. This trend is likely to continue; for example, Minnesota has recently added a requirement that in order to be an approved supervisor for licensing purposes, licensees must have completed thirty hours of training in supervision and that all supervisors must obtain continuing education in supervision every two years. These new requirements for supervisors come at the same time that many appli-cants and licensees are having difficulties finding qualified supervisors in the first place. Now, though, as we saw in the previous section the use of technology makes contact possible at a distance; given the shortage of qual-ified supervisors in some areas, this new mode of access to supervision could prove a valuable alternative. It brings its own challenges, though, particularly for regulators. NASW's Legal Issues of the Month (April 17, 2009) presents the issue succinctly:

> Rural social workers may find that electronic supervision is a means to meet licensing board requirements. Rural states that have not made allowance for this type of supervisory arrangement may need to consider amending their regulations or laws in order to facilitate the appropriate training of sufficient numbers of new social workers into the profession.

Involuntary dynamics also are likely increasingly to affect licensing supervision as the proportion of social work clients who are involuntary continues to rise (Bibus & Jud, 2009; Rooney, 2009; Trotter, 1999). More and more people find themselves under court order or other less-formal pressures to have contact with social workers (e.g., in situations involving child maltreatment or domestic violence, or in circumstances where seeking assessment and services is a prerequisite for benefits such as attending job training sessions in order to receive public assistance). Despite the need for more careful supervision of social work with vulnerable people who have little choice but to work with the supervisee, attention to case consultation and to the educational and supportive functions of supervision is less possible as administrative duties continue to increase and consume the role. Moreover, in small grassroots neighborhood agencies, it is less likely that qualified supervisors will be available for licensees. And in some host settings such as in health care, social workers' supervisors come from other professions and disciplinary backgrounds. In fact, social workers may increasingly witness their positions being taken over by other professionals.

The End of Social Work as a Distinct Profession?

Another "hot" issue is the emergence of other disciplines seeking professional status whose licensure may pose a threat to social workers; the existence of these other professionals may confuse those who use social services to an even greater degree than current variations in social work regulation do. Alert to this potential threat, leadership of the Association of Baccalaureate Social Work Directors set up a special Hot Topic Session at the November 2009 Annual Program Meeting of the CSWE. This session aimed to develop a unified response to initiatives seeking regulation of human service professionals, psychiatric rehabilitation specialists, and other practitioners whose scope of practice includes activities ordinarily performed by social workers. Organizers of the special session saw these new trends in licensing as potentially "derailing" social work and social work education, especially BSW programs, because credentialing other professions to practice in the same domains as social workers practice both duplicates services and confuses consumers.

For years, the similarities between social work education and courses in human services have been noticed. Differences have been observed as well, such as the lack of one uniform set of accrediting standards for human services contrasted with the CSWE's long-standing prominence in accreditation of social work programs in the United States. With field education recognized as the signature pedagogy in the discipline, social work students also must complete a more rigorous practicum than human service majors typically experience. On the one hand, social workers ground their practice on widely accepted and commonly held core values and ethical principles. On the other hand, human service professionals tend to have had more interdisciplinary content in their educational programs and to be more eclectic in background and approaches to practice. Moreover, people and communities currently underserved by social work, often disproportionately from oppressed groups, must rely on other disciplines in addition to social work to meet their needs, and these clients have a right to benefit from the minimum standards and protections provided through regulation of all of their helping professionals.

Still, licensing human service professionals could siphon away candidates from social work programs and practice. In sectors of practice such as child welfare and aging services, BSW practitioners form the backbone of the workforce. Because social work is established as a licensed profession, BSW programs have thrived in many of the states that offer BSW graduates the opportunity to practice in an officially sanctioned capacity. However, if less-rigorous and less-expensive paths to licensed practice for undergraduates become available, will prospective social work students turn instead to other professional studies?

Disaster Response

One of social work's strengths is the competency social workers have to coordinate other disciplines and community resources to address human needs. The role of service coordination is particularly valuable in response to disasters and emergencies such as devastating tsunamis, typhoons and hurricanes, pandemics, and acts of war or terrorism. The National Response Framework established by the federal government (USDHS, 2008) calls for planned and integrated participation by national and local government and private agencies and organizations in responding to such disasters. "Given this recent change in policy, social workers and other community workers can expect to play a greater role in the development of local disaster response policy and structures" (Schock & Bosch, in press). When disasters and other emergencies occur, states affected have realized that there need to be mechanisms for licensed practitioners from other states to be authorized quickly and smoothly to be allowed to practice. Regulators are likely to revise current rules and legislation to better accommodate emergency responders. See box 4.3 for Minnesota's legislative provision for a temporary license; the practice act also provides for an inactive license status variance to allow provision of emergency services by licensees on temporary leave or emeritus licensees (MS 148D.075 Subd. 6[b]). The need for a nationally coordinated response capacity may encourage more reciprocity across state lines in the near future. The example set

---

Box 4.3 2009 Minnesota Statutes 148D.060 Temporary Licenses

Subd. 2. Emergency situations and persons currently licensed in another jurisdiction.

The board may issue a temporary license to practice social work to an applicant who is licensed or credentialed to practice social work in another jurisdiction, may or may not have applied for a license under section 148D.055, and has:

(1) applied for a temporary license on a form provided by the board;

(2) submitted a form provided by the board authorizing the board to complete a criminal background check;

(3) submitted evidence satisfactory to the board that the applicant is currently licensed or credentialed to practice social work in another jurisdiction;

(4) attested on a form provided by the board that the applicant has completed the requirements for a baccalaureate or graduate degree in social work from a program accredited by the Council on Social Work Education, the Canadian Association of Schools of Social Work, or a similar accreditation body designated by the board; and

(5) not engaged in conduct that was or would be in violation of the standards of practice specified in sections 148D.195 to 148D.240. If the applicant has engaged in conduct that was or would be in violation of the standards of practice, the board may take action pursuant to sections 148D.255 to 148D.270.

---

among social workers and other community organizers in Asia will be instructive (e.g., Tan, 2009; Tan & Rowlands, 2008).

Lack of Empirical Data: How Do We Know If Licensure Is Achieving Its Purposes?

Students often express surprise over sanctions having been handed out to licensed social workers found to be in violation of licensing codes or the NASW Code of Ethics. In a perfect world, one might believe that licensed social workers or those who have been deemed "competent" to practice would not commit infractions against clients or the profession. However, we must realize that social workers are people, and people make mistakes. We should be wary of placing too much emphasis on the person and more emphasis on the process of regulation to see if we are actually achieving our goal of ensuring competence through practice regulation.

Because licensing is meant to protect the public from incompetent social workers, one might argue that we can tell whether this goal is being achieved through the presence or absence of reports of ethical or licensing code violations. With this in mind, we turn to an examination of the literature on evaluating social work codes of ethics violations historically and efforts to examine licensing violation sanctions during more recent years. (It is important to remember here that the standards of conduct specified in licensing statutes, though often based on NASW's Code of Ethics, are different, usually more prescriptive and less aspirational than NASW's Code of Ethics.)

Early efforts to examine sanctions against social workers used results of adjudication efforts against NASW members as the source of data. For example, McCann and Cutler (1979) utilized NASW ethics cases between 1956 and 1977 (n = 154) to better understand what the adjudication process and experience had been like for the NASW. Because of the adjudication process utilized by NASW at the time, the researchers used only data from one category of complaints—those involving "complaints against members for alleged unethical conduct" (p. 5). However, several pieces of notable information were gained from this review. For example, double-digit reports were made during 1970 and between 1973 and 1977, for a total of 107, or a majority of the 154 cases. The greatest number of adjudicated cases involved "contested firings" (36) and what were labeled "violations of personnel practices" (22) (p. 6). Furthermore, of the total number of cases, manager complaints against employees (n = 81) were the most frequently stated relationship between the person making the complaint and the social worker. The second-most frequently noted relationship occurred between colleagues (n = 22), with the third occurring between the client and the worker (n = 21) (p. 7). The researchers noted also that there were instances where a report of inappropriate behavior was filed against the worker by another party, in which the second party may not have been able to clearly identify specific parts of the code that had been violated. Out of this study came a call for social workers to become more familiar with NASW's Code of Ethics and for some effective process that could be utilized to resolve complaints more effectively.

Berliner (1989) examined 292 cases that had reached the highest appellate level of the NASW National Committee on Inquiry following hearings at the local jurisdiction between 1979 and 1985. His review revealed that

[h]alf of the 10 jurisdictions most active with COI [Committee on Inquiry] issues lacked social work regulation, including the state that reported the most cases. In fact, two of the top three in complaint frequency represented

unregulated jurisdictions. There were no data, however, to identify any causal relationship. (p. 69)

In addition, Berliner (1989) found that colleagues were willing to report what they considered to be ethical violations on the part of other colleagues: this occurred in 162 (55 percent) of the cases reviewed. Private agencies were more likely to have initiated reports than were public agencies. Most of the sexual assault cases filed were filed against private practitioners. Among the suggestions noted by the author were a "database that would enable systematic study of ethical infractions" (p. 70) and a shortening of the process by which cases would be heard.

During the 1990s, NASW performed an in-house review of cases adjudicated between 1982 and 1992. Using a randomized sample of 300 cases finalized during this ten-year period, the association found that filings against members for infractions against clients had increased over previous years, with "sexual activities with clients" being "the largest category (29.2%)" (Boland-Prom, 2009, p. 352).

When also taking a look at NASW Code of Ethics violations that resulted in misconduct findings, Strom-Gottfried (2000) examined data from 1986 to 1997 and reported on frequencies, types of misconduct, and final disposition of cases. From 267 cases, the researcher noted a total of 781 different violations across ten different categories. Categories listed included boundary violations, poor practice, competence, record keeping, honesty, breach of confidentiality, informed consent, collegial violations, billing, and conflicts of interest. The category with the largest number of reports was that of boundary violations, of which 254 were cited. The two largest subcategories of boundary violations were recorded as sexual activity with clients (107) and dual relationships (77). ("Dual relationship violations" are conflicts of interest wherein the social worker takes on a second role with a client or former client that exploits the client or in other ways harms the client.) The second-largest of the ten categories referenced was that of "poor practice" (160), which the author defined as "a variety of areas in which the services offered by the social worker fell short of accepted standards" (p. 254). Included were areas such as "failure to use accepted skills" (41), "premature termination" (33), "poor case transfer or case referral" (30), and "prolonged care" (24). The author noted that changes in the NASW Code of Ethics that resulted in an expansion of standards since the time of the study would help "strengthen practice and enhance adjudication in a number of ways" (p. 260).

Building on the previous works, Strom-Gottfried (2003) continued with an examination of NASW Code of Ethics violations between 1986 and 1997 and offered a comparison of the findings with the NASW membership data as well as with other studies of this nature. For this review, the author reviewed a total of 894 cases filed between mid-1986 and the end of 1997. She found that 50 percent of those against whom cases were filed were licensed or certified in their state; however, this number could be higher because there were approximately 36 percent of respondents whose license or certification status was not known. The proportion of men and private practitioners among the subjects of the complaints was also notable:

> This study indicates that men were found responsible for almost half of the cases in which there were Code violations–more than twice their representation in the NASW membership. It also indicates that although private practitioners appear to be the subject of complaints to a lesser degree than their proportion in the membership, when they are accused they are found to have committed violations at a much higher rate than their agency or university counterparts. (Strom-Gottfried, 2003, p. 93)

In one state (Texas), Daley and Doughty (2006, 2007) conducted a study of complaints against BSW- and MSW-licensed social workers that had been investigated by the Texas State Board of Social Work Examiners from 1995 to 2003. Out of the 1,272 allegations of unethical practice during this period, 18.2 percent of the complaints involved BSW practitioners, 23.3 percent involved MSW practitioners, and 58.5 percent involved clinical social work practitioners. (These allegations included both substantiated and unfounded complaints.) The authors analyzed the complaints with categories developed by Strom-Gottfried (2000). Looking at 276 substantiated cases of violations of NASW's Code of Ethics (mostly involving MSW practitioners), Strom-Gottfried categorized the complaints as follows:

Violating Boundaries	32.4%
Poor Practice	20.4%
Competence	12.0%
Record Keeping	8.9%
Honesty	6.5%
Confidentiality	5.2%
Informed Consent	4.7%
Collegial Actions	4.2%
Reimbursement	2.9%
Conflicts of Interest	2.8%

For comparison, Daley and Doughty's (2007) findings (from their Tables 2 & 3) were as follows:

	BSWs	MSWs	Clinical Social Workers
Boundary Issues	16.9%	16.8%	24.6%
Poor Practice	25.9%	20.9%	21.4%
Competency	9.1%	9.1%	7.0%
Record Keeping	6.1%	2.4%	5.2%
Honesty	16.4%	21.9%	9.3%
Confidentiality	3.5%	7.7%	12.2%
Informed Consent	6.1%	4.0%	4.7%
Billing	5.6%	4.7%	4.8%
Conflict of Interests	10.4%	12.5%	10.8%

We can see that for BSW and MSW generalist practitioners, poor practice was a more common category of complaint than were boundary issues, which were the most common category for clinical and NASW practitioners. Poor practice included direct service delivery problems or omission of basic standard services at initial assessment, during contact with clients, or at termination. These could result from inadequate preparation or training. (If poor service was the result of the practitioner's impairment, though, the complaint was categorized under competence.) Examples of poor practice included inappropriate treatment and termination, disrespect for self-determination, and mistreatment.

Two thirds of the boundary issues involved dual relationships of a financial or personal nature during which the social worker was alleged to have exploited the client. Note also that the category of honesty contained a higher proportion of complaints against generalist practitioners than against clinical practitioners, whereas complaints against clinical practitioners often fell into the category of confidentiality. Honesty violations involve fraud, falsification of records, or misrepresentation of credentials. Record keeping complaints also involve inaccurate or withheld information.

In their article published online reporting on this study, the authors proceed to an intriguing discussion of the differential risk that social workers may face ethically depending on their job functions and the settings within which they practice. If, for example, social workers work in highly structured employment settings such as public agencies, where there are more likely to be more formal rules about handling confidential information, perhaps the risk of confidential violations is reduced. Employment in public settings may mean social workers have more involuntary clients, and the risk for complaints about either poor practice or honesty might be expected to be elevated (Section 5, 10th paragraph). They recommend emphasizing use of supervision and consultation during social work courses and continuing education opportunities, particularly in dealing with advocacy dilemmas that can arise when, with the best of intentions, we are tempted to slant or shape information so that clients are deemed eligible for services we believe they need.

Most recently, Boland-Prom analyzed a sample of complaints against licensees in 27 states (including Texas) from 1999 ro 2004 and found that almost one quarter of the complaints were in the category of dual relationships and boundary violations (2009, p. 357). She also noted that several states do not require criminal background checks and that there is inconsistency across states in the degree of sanctions applied to licencees who have "inappropriate physical or sexual contact with minors" (p. 359).

Limitations with Historical Reviews

As with many pieces of research, limitations existed in each of the aforementioned reviews of data. For example, many of these studies used the NASW records of violations. This means that violations that occurred or were resolved without the involvement of the NASW were most probably not accounted for. In addition, for the most part these studies do not indicate whether or not the persons against whom complaints were filed were licensed social workers. What we do know is that there were members of NASW who were found in violation of the NASW Code of Ethics, which in many cases may not be identical to states' regulatory practice codes.

McCann and Cutler (1979) analyze data from one category, while they do not examine two other categories at all. The reason these categories were not examined is because they dealt more with complaints against agencies than with complaints against specific individuals. In addition, data were only collected for this review when certain guidelines had been followed. Again, this may have limited an examination of the full scope of adjudication at that time.

In the Berliner (1989) examination of NASW complaints, data were gathered only for those cases where certain criteria had been met and complainants had decided to pursue an appeal to the National Committee on Inquiry (NCOI). Again, this meant that not all violations were reported in the 292 cases examined. In addition, though 292 physical cases were examined, there may have been more than one violation per case.

Strom-Gottfried (2000, 2003) reviewed larger numbers of violations than earlier studies, and information regarding license or certification status was obtained. However, Strom-Gottfried notes that no data were gathered on those cases where resolution occurred within the respondent's jurisdiction; therefore, the findings (though more comprehensive) may have still been somewhat incomplete. Finally, Daley and Doughty's study (2006 & 2007) building on Strom-Gottfried's work includes data from just one state; replication in other states would be informative.

Are We Getting It Right, Now?

As the regulation movement grew across this country, so too did challenges to examining the effectiveness of licensure. Two of these challenges are the growing number of licensees and the unequal licensing structure that exists in this country. As a result of the move toward professional regulation, licensing infractions are dealt with at the state level rather than at the national level of jurisdiction and data are collected by ASWB rather by NASW. Notably, the change from one entity to another may have led to gaps in data collection, although, since 2000, the Disciplinary Action Reporting System (DARS) has been used to capture reporting and adjudication data.

ASWB's Troy Elliott (personal communication, 2009) reports,

> according to our latest dues totals, there are about 383,000 licensees in the U.S., and that includes California. With Canada, the total is 404,000. The DARS system contains 4822 actions taken against 3570 social workers, and that does include a fairly small number of Canadian jurisdictions/actions.

While the number of social workers against whom action has been taken is low comparatively speaking (in Canada, 3,570 actions versus 404,000 licensees; in the United States, 4,822 actions versus 383,000 licensees—in both cases approximately 1 percent of the total number of licensed social workers at this time), what we do not know is how many of the social workers who were subject to the actions passed multiple-choice exams to get their licenses, and whether this smaller number is indicative of what may actually be a larger problem.

Simply stated, even if we could agree on a single definition of competence, multiple-choice tests would not test for competency at all points in time. In addition, as was raised by Middleman (1984), "The final areas of concern are with the quality of the assessment instruments and the instruments' relation to competence in social work practice" (p. 151). Many pieces of similar feedback were provided in response to Boutté-Queen's (2003) inquiry some twenty years after Middleman's statement when respondents said the following:

> "In spite of minimum requirements and testing there is not assurance of competency in social work any [sic] more than there is in the AMA." (p. 210)
> "Licensing does not make a better social worker. Knowledge and passion and love of my clients and for [sic] the profession does" (p. 210)
> It's unrealistic to believe that a social worker's competency can be measured by passing a test alone. Reputation, skill, commitment are more important than being able to pass a test." (p. 210)

When it comes to assessing whether we are meeting our goals with licensure, the second challenge that compounds the growth in numbers of licensees and thus potential infractions is the confusing licensing structure in the United States. Because there are currently more than twenty acronyms that represent various levels of licensing, the tasks of assessing competence and violations to code become somewhat overwhelming. Combine this with the presence of different licensing codes of ethics and standards of conduct for each state and a data collection nightmare looms. However, these challenges should be viewed more as opportunities for improvement than as barriers to successful evaluation efforts.

Students are told over and over to evaluate: look at the implemented action, intervention, policy, and so on, and see if it is actually working. To date, for a number of reasons, evaluation has not been fully undertaken to find out if licensure is actually achieving its purpose. Therefore, it is exciting to see that, in 2009, after years of discussion about licensure effectiveness, the ASWB has recently begun looking at ways to capture information about whether licensure is achieving its purposes. Under their Research Grant Program, a part of the American Foundation for Research and Consumer Education in Social Work Regulation, funds have been provided for researchers to "explore the ways in which professional social work regulation impacts the profession and the public it serves" (from the application form on ASWB's website). Specifically, proposals that address research focused on continuing education models, what students and social practitioners know about licensure, faculty and consumer awareness of licensure, best practices, and complaint analyses were accepted through May 31, 2009. It is hoped that the findings from research of this nature will enable us to better understand licensure and its effect on social work practice and client services.

CHAPTER FIVE

Conclusion: The Role of Regulation in Our Profession

THIS PRIMER HAS INTRODUCED students to the role of regulation in the practice of social work. Every state in the United States now regulates social workers. Lawmakers have determined that it is in the interests of the public to hold social workers accountable to a set of minimum standards of practice and conduct, and to investigate and address complaints if their practice falls below those standards. Although states' policies and procedures for licensing social workers vary in sometimes confusing ways, the fundamental steps required to become a licensed social worker in any state usually include completing an accredited program in social work education, passing an examination demonstrating requisite knowledge, submitting required documentation, and showing continuing or growing competence and compliance with standards through supervision, continuing education, and renewal.

In chapter 1, we reviewed the development of licensing policies in the United States and witnessed the role of professional associations, in particular the National Association of Social Workers (NASW), in advocating for licensure. Like all policies, licensing regulations for social workers can have outcomes that are predicted and intended, and they can have outcomes that are neither. Outcomes in either case can be positive or negative for social workers, their clients, or the public. A particular outcome (such as access to an independent board for clients whose social workers' practice has fallen below standards) would be welcomed by social workers, clients, and the public. Other outcomes (such as a shortage of credentialed practitioners available to serve people in vulnerable circumstances) could have negative effects on clients and the public while working to the financial advantage or enhanced professional status of some social workers. There have been a few studies examining outcomes of licensing policies, but we do not know enough about whether regulating social workers is resulting in good services for clients as intended or whether unintended consequences such as a reduction in access to social work services have resulted.

As with many public policies, establishment and development of professional licensing across the helping disciplines historically have not been dependent on proof of effectiveness. Nevertheless, continuing research will be a fruitful resource for improvements in regulations. Certainly, in our mobile society more uniformity across the state and interstate agreements that reduce disruption in services and facilitate service access for both practitioners and clients are in order. In chapter 2, we presented and discussed a framework for systematic analysis of licensing policies that promised to assist in the assessment of current policies and procedures and to lay the groundwork for such improvements. We have offered several examples of how this framework might prove useful, including comparative analysis across states and nations.

Chapter 3 provided descriptions of the distinctive regulatory landscapes in the United Kingdom, selected countries from Asia, and India, plus brief overviews of the status of social work licensing in Canada and Mexico. Thus, evident variations in regulations and indeed the very definition of social work practice present a challenge to the intended public protection purpose of licensing. Using the SW-PIE (Profession(al)-in-Environment) perspective, we explored a sampling of several challenging issues, debates, and controversies regarding social work licensure in chapter 4. For example, while social work education and social work educators have championed licensing for social workers and in many countries have taken the lead in establishing standards of practice, the U.S. Council on Social Work Education (CSWE) opposes mandatory licensing of social work educators.

Roles of Education, Professional Associations, and Regulation

The CSWE's position on licensing faculty illustrates one way that the roles of educational programs and accreditation, professional associations, and regulation are not identical. Social work education focuses on establishing, encouraging, supporting, maintaining, and developing high-quality programs in which students learn the knowledge and skills (i.e., the competencies) required for social work practice. Students come to recognize the degree to which their core values are congruent with the values of the social work profession, and most join with their professors in making a commitment to those values and to lifelong learning. Social work graduates often turn to the programs of social work education for consultation on cases and policies, discourse on urgent issues, help with research and evaluation, planning for improvements in service delivery, and continuing development of their competencies in order to hone their practice to meet contemporary and future needs. The CSWE's mission statement aptly describes the role of education and accreditation of educational programs:

> CSWE aims to promote and strengthen the quality of social work education through preparation of competent social work professionals by providing national leadership and a forum for collective action. CSWE pursues this mission through setting and maintaining policy and program standards, accrediting bachelor's and master's degree programs in social work, promoting research and faculty development, and advocating for social work education. (http://www.cswe.org/CSWE/Aboutaspx)

Thus, the CSWE is a professional association, formed and governed by social work professional educators. The association has more than 3,000 individual members from nearly 700 BSW and MSW programs. Other professional associations, in particular the NASW, collaborate with CSWE. In fact, the purpose of social work and definition of social work practice developed by NASW in the NASW Code of Ethics are incorporated into the educational policy and standards set by CSWE. NASW and the other professional associations (see appendix B) directly represent, serve, and advocate for the interests of members: individual social workers. For example, NASW's website describes the association as follows:

> The National Association of Social Workers (NASW) is the largest membership organization of professional social workers in the world, with 150,000 members. NASW works to enhance the professional growth and development of its members, to create and maintain professional standards, and to advance sound social policies. . . . NASW's primary functions include promoting the professional development of its members, establishing and maintaining professional standards of practice, advancing sound social policies, and providing services that protect its members and enhance their professional status. (https://www.socialworkers.org/)

Students often are members of NASW and other professional associations, sometimes exercising leadership in carrying out member services, policy making, and advocacy. As we discussed in the last chapter, being a member of professional associations imparts many benefits for a social worker, from opportunities for networking and venues for continuing education to support for promotion of ethical standards and integrity and political mobilization in the interests of social work.

Both educational programs and professional associations have played critical roles in promoting licensure of social workers in every state and have taken the lead in advocating for regulation of social work practice both nationally and internationally. Indeed, in some countries the professional associations and educators constitute the regulatory body setting practice standards and holding social workers accountable to them (e.g., Canada and India). But in the United States, NASW standards apply only to members. CSWE's accreditation standards apply only to member programs. And both students and practitioners often make the mistaken assumption that because licensing is promoted and supported for the most part by the professional associations of which they are members and which primarily serve their interests, licensing boards are likewise oriented to provide benefits to licensees. Many are disappointed to discover that "social workers don't get anything from the Board for their licensing fee!" (a common complaint discussed in Luinenburg et al., 2002, p. 16). As is by now clear to readers, boards regulating social work practice do not focus primarily on providing benefits to licensees or the profession of social work; rather, they are set up to establish a legally defensible set of standards of practice and conduct to which licensees are held accountable, and to respond to reports that an individual's practice has not met those standards or that a person is practicing unlawfully (i.e., without a license).

Moreover, regulatory boards assume prerogatives and powers in order to carry out this public protection mandate that can trump the policies and positions of educational accreditation and professional associations. This is because CSWE and NASW, for example, are private entities, and the principle of delegation of powers reserves to public government bodies the final say in matters of public protection. As explained in ASWB's commentary on its Model Social Work Practice Act (p. 16), "it is a well-established rule of administrative law that any delegation of governmental power must carry with it appropriate limitations and procedural safeguards for affected individuals." Thus, social work regulatory boards have reserved the right to define what is minimally acceptable social work practice as well as what knowledge and skills licensees must have learned in their educational programs. Even though regulatory boards were established by legislation often advocated for and frequently written by members of NASW and CSWE, boards can and do at times take positions that may be contrary to those taken by the professional associations. And, as licensing fees rise, members of professional associations are faced with having to decide between maintaining their membership or their license; invariably, if forced to choose one over the other, social workers will choose to maintain their license. Thankfully, many social workers have rejected this forced choice because they see it in their interests as professionals to maintain both membership in associations and their license.

For their part, regulatory boards will usually cultivate collaboration with the professionals whose practice comes under their jurisdiction rather than turn prematurely to more adversarial positions. Encouragement, persuasion, and education tend to work better than threats and punitive measures in protecting public interests. After all, boards of social work, professional associations, social work education programs, and social work practitioners share the ultimate goal of fostering the highest-quality client services possible.

Professional Social Work

"Licensure has replaced the academic degree as a measure of minimum competence" (Doelling, 1997, p. 169).

As social work graduates embark on their professional journeys, they will likely want or need to become licensed.

Preparing for licensure upon completion of a social work degree is no different than preparing for licensure or certification upon graduation from education, law, or health care disciplines. Licensure is a professional responsibility and, in most cases, is not optional. (Luinenburg et al., 2002, p. 17)

Even if prospective employers might not require an employee to be licensed, the regulatory board probably will; boards have jurisdiction over individual social workers, but not usually over agencies or employers. Therefore, students are advised to begin preparing for their license well before they graduate. Most board members and staff are delighted to come to campus to meet with prospective applicants, and most boards have informative websites and other resources to guide students who want to become licensed. (See ASWB's website for links to local boards.) If students have difficulty with multiple-choice standardized test formats, they may find useful a short course in preparing to take the licensing examination. Many local NASW chapters offer such courses and other supports to help applicants do as well as possible on the examinations. Reviewing basic methods and human-behavior-in-the-social-environment (HBSE) texts is another effective strategy.

If an applicant does not pass the examination, we recommend consultation with mentors who know the applicant's learning style well. The chances of passing the examination on retaking it without improved preparation are slim. A mentor can help in developing preparation strategies that are more likely to lead either to success in passing the examination or to reconsideration of whether a career as a licensed social worker is a good fit. ASWB has developed a number of resources; their tips for improving one's score in retaking the examination (usually after an at least ninety-day waiting period) state, "Reassessing your social work knowledge . . . and conducting an honest appraisal of your weaknesses and strengths may well put you on the road to success with the examination" (ASWB, 2010a).

Some applicants for whom English is a second learned language, or others whose educational foundation in elementary and high school was disrupted or substandard, have experienced difficulties in passing the examination. They may have had stellar records in their social work programs and have been evaluated by their professors and other licensed social workers as manifestly competent in social work practice. Yet, even on retaking the examination after extensive and intensive preparation, they do not pass it and thus cannot be licensed. Recognizing this circumstance, some states either have developed or are looking into alternative routes to licensure that do not entail passing ASWB's standardized national examination. The thinking is that if there are other defensible means for ensuring that candidates have basic social work competencies, it is better for the residents of the state to have access to a more diverse range of licensed social workers whose practice is then under the ongoing regulation of boards to which clients can turn should practice or competencies fall below standards. These procedures have been initiated and supported on the mobilized advocacy of students, faculty, licensed practitioners, professional associations, client groups, and other constituencies. This is a good example of the value of joining with others in influencing, in this case, regulatory policies (see, for example, Alexander & Johnston, 2008).

Ideally, the process of applying for licensure will provide students with a formal opportunity to reflect on what it means to be a social worker, and how their life decisions have been and will be congruent with fundamental social work values and ethical principles. The social work license can be a prominent symbol of the "habit of mind" (Konopka, 1958, p. 9) that is the hallmark of professional social work. Hence, the application process and initial license are just the beginning phases of a potentially lifelong relationship between students and regulatory boards. Combined with the significant rapport most students have with their educational programs and their membership in professional associations, their relationship with the regulatory system constitutes the lattice on which their social work careers will grow. Particularly as members of professional associations, they will be able to exert influence on regulations and their implementation. Additionally, licensees may find service on boards of social work personally as well as professionally rewarding. (One of the authors of this primer, Bibus, considers his work for the Minnesota Board of Social Work to be among the most fulfilling of his professional life.) Other dual licenses and certifications may also be worth pursuing as they develop specialties in their practice; see Doelling (1997) and appendix B for examples.

As noted above, regulatory boards do not focus primarily on serving social workers, although their public protection mission certainly can benefit us. However, professional associations do exist primarily to serve members. Luinenburg and colleagues (2002, pp. 30–31) list nine ways that professional associations address workplace and professional issues:

1. Profession Building (upholding standards, educating the public, building pride)
2. Workplace Issues (focusing on hiring, salaries, and working conditions)
3. Macro Change, Including Legislative (lobbying, shaping, influencing policies)
4. Improving Practice (supporting research, evaluation, scholarship, publications)
5. Social Justice (advocating for positive changes in systems that affect lives)
6. Licensure Requirements (offering continuing education, supervision resources)
7. Personal Services (providing job leads, insurance, etc.)
8. Newsletters (offering news on what's happening within the profession)
9. Networking (facilitating all of the above!)

Luinenburg and colleagues (2002) conclude with the observation that "many social workers choose to join several associations." Our dues are an investment in social work and in the highest-quality services possible for our clients. Thus, professional associations' (and education's) role focuses beyond the minimum standards set by regulatory boards. The authors of this primer highly value our active participation in local, national, and international associations, including NASW, NABSW, CSWE, AASWG, BPD, and other associations at the local level.

For social workers in employment settings where there is collective bargaining, labor unions play an important role in supporting professional practice. Like professional associations, unions serve the interests of their members. Using the power of group solidarity, unions negotiate and advocate for decent wages, compensation, benefits, safe and healthy workplace conditions, fair performance evaluation and promotion procedures, and other rights for their members and all the employees they represent. Unions can assert effective influence on legislative and regulatory policies. Unions representing social workers have tended to oppose mandatory licensing as an impingement on their members' autonomy and as a potential interference with or threat to their livelihoods. However, since unions are governed by members, social workers can as members influence the union to ensure that licensing has indirect benefits for members and for their clients. As we noted earlier in citing Karger (1988), social workers who are not licensed could be perceived as offering second-class services. The power of union advocacy could be tapped to support (or at least not oppose) the licensing of all social workers as a means to strengthen the professional status of employees relative to other licensed professions.

More Than a Job

Like many students, we (the authors) were drawn to social work because we wanted to help people. ("Interest in helping people" was the top-ranked factor influencing the career choice of social workers responding to NASW's 2007 workforce survey; Whitaker, 2009, pp. 9–10.) What we witnessed social workers doing on the job—for example, when I (Bibus) met the social workers who were helping the youngsters who lived at the group home where I was assistant director in 1970 or when I (Boutté-Queen), at twelve years of age, first saw social workers referenced as service providers to children overseas on a card that came in the mail—seemed to be meaningful work. As do our students today, we resonated with the core values of social work: "service, social justice, the dignity and worth of the person, the importance of human relationships, integrity, competence, human rights, and scientific inquiry" (CSWE, 2008, EP 1.1; see also NASW's Code of Ethics, 2008). When we began practicing as social workers, we soon learned that we were not performing our duties in isolation but rather as part of agencies and a team of colleagues, supervisors, and, most importantly, our clients. Our work emerged in relationships on behalf of services with clients, caring relationships as social work professionals in the environment (SW-PIE). We came to see that a career as a social worker transcended any given job, position, or employment. We became part of a profession. Social work did not stop when we came home from the work-place. We discovered that, try as we might, our efforts as individuals to effect positive changes with people, policies, and systems were quite lim-ited. However, joining with others in the profession, especially as members and leaders of professional associations, we could play a part in bringing about substantial and lasting improvements in people's lives, including our own. Through educational preparation, we built on strengths of character and personal talents to contribute to the mission of the profession of social work, and we hope to continue to do so for the rest of our lives.

Thus, for us social work is not just a job, not just a career, not even just a profession, but rather is a vocation in the deepest sense of the word: it is a calling to give and care for others and this world as we have been given to and cared for. Being a social worker and teaching social work tap gifts and talents as fully as we can imagine; hence our professional roles are profoundly meaningful and fulfilling. Writing this primer has deepened our appreciation for the role of regulations and the regulatory system—complex, various, and imperfect as they are in our professional lives. By encoding and reinforcing standards of professional practice, conduct, and ethics, licensing provides a legal infrastructure on which to hold ourselves and to be held accountable. So, we end here remembering a quotation read by Lynn Ellingson, graduate admissions staff at Augsburg College in Minneapolis, at information sessions for prospective MSW students, defining "vocation" as

The place God calls you to is the place
where your deep gladness and
the world's deep hunger meet. (Buechner, 1973, p. 95)

References

Abo-El-Nasr, M. M. (1997). Egypt. In N. S. Mayadas, T. D. Watts, & D. Elliot (Eds.), *International handbook on social work theory and practice* (pp. 205–222). Westport, CT: Greenwood Press.

Adams, K. B., Matto, H. C., & LeCroy, C. W. (2009). Limitations of evidence-based practice for social work education: Unpacking the complexity. *Journal of Social Work Education, 4*(2), 165–186.

Agostinelli, A. J. (1973). *Legal regulation of social work.* Washington, DC: NASW.

Aguilar, M. A. (1997). Mexico. In N. S. Mayadas, T. D. Watts, & D. Elliot (Eds.), *International handbook on social work theory and practice* (pp. 60–75). Westport, CT: Greenwood Press.

Albert, R. (2000). *Law and social work practice* (2nd ed.). New York: Springer Publishing.

Alexander, L., & Johnston, B. (2008). *Final report on alternative paths to licensure for the Minnesota Board of Social Work.* Minneapolis, MN: Minnesota Board of Social Work. Available at http://www.socialwork.state.mn.us/.

American Association of State Social Work Boards (AASSWB). (1996). *Social work job analysis in support of the American Association of State Social Work Board Examination Program: Final report.* Culpepper, VA: Author.

Arne, R. F. (1952). Protection of the public through licensing of social workers. *Social Work Journal, 33*(4), 184–190.

Association of Social Work Boards (ASWB). (2002). Panel speaks: But faculty licensure discussion illustrates lack of unified voice. *ASWB Association News, 12*(3), 1–2, 4.

Association of Social Work Boards (ASWB). (2004). *Analysis of the practice of social work: 2003.* Culpeper, VA: Author. Available at www.aswb.org.

Association of Social Work Boards (ASWB). (2007a). *Model Social Work Practice Act.* Culpeper, VA: Author. Available at www.aswb.org.

Association of Social Work Boards (ASWB). (2007b). *Social work laws and regulations: A comparison guide.* Culpeper, VA: Author. Available at www.aswb.org.

Association of Social Work Boards (ASWB). (2008a). ASWB exam gets high marks from outside audit. *ASWB Association News, 18*(5), 2, 6. Available at http://www.aswb.org/pdfs/ASWBNews1008.pdf.

Association of Social Work Boards (ASWB). (2008b). ESL—lots of questions, very few answers: ASWB task force struggles with the absence of data. *ASWB Association News, 18*(5), 5–6. Available at http://www.aswb.org/pdfs/ASWB News1008.pdf.

Association of Social Work Boards (ASWB). (2009a). ASWB's examination committee has new members. *ASWB Association News, 19*(2), 6.

Association of Social Work Boards (ASWB). (2009b). *An analysis of supervision for social work licensure: Guidelines on supervision for regulators and educators.* Culpeper, VA: Author.

Association of Social Work Boards (ASWB). (2009c). After eight years, time for an increase? *ASWB Association News, 19*(4).

Association of Social Work Boards (ASWB). (2010a). Common concerns about the ASWB social work licensing exam. Available at www.aswb.org.

Association of Social Work Boards (ASWB). (2010b). 2010 analysis of the practice of social work. Culpeper, VA: Author.

Association of Social Work Boards (ASWB). (2010c). Social work laws and regulations data base. Data Tables: Available at www.aswb.org.

Barker, R. L., & Branson, D. M. (2000). *Forensic social work: Legal aspects of professional practice* (2nd ed.). New York: Haworth Press.

Barretta-Herman, A. (2008). Meeting the expectations of the global standards. *International Social Work, 51*(6), 823–834.

Berliner, A. K. (1989). Misconduct in social work practice. *Social Work, 39,* 69–72.

Bibus, A. A. (1993). In pursuit of the missing link: The influence of supervision on social workers' practice with involuntary clients. *The Clinical Supervisor, 11*(2), 7–22.

Bibus, A. A. (1995). Reflections on social work from Cuernavaca, Mexico. *International Social Work, 38*(3), 243–252.

Bibus, A. A. (November, 2007). *Destination deferred: A report to the Minnesota Board of Social Work on the exemption from mandatory licensing for social workers in Minnesota county social services.* Available under "Board Reports" at http://www.socialwork.state.mn.us/.

Bibus, A. A., & Jud, C. (2009). Applying the involuntary perspective to supervision. In R. H. Rooney, *Strategies for work with involuntary clients* (2nd ed.) (pp. 424–448). New York: Columbia University Press.

Bibus, A. A., & Link, R. J. (1999). Global approaches to learning social welfare policy. In C. S. Ramanathan & R. J. Link, *All our futures: Principles and resources for social work practice in a global era* (pp. 94–120). Belmont, CA: Wadsworth Publishing Company.

Biggerstaff, M. A. (1992). Evaluating the reliability of oral examinations for licensure of clinical social workers in Virginia. *Research on Social Work Practice, 4*(4), 481–197.

Biggerstaff, M. A. (1995). Licensing, regulation, and certification. In R. L. Edwards, Editor-in-Chief, *The encyclopedia of social work* (19th ed., Vol. 2, pp. 1616–1624). Washington, DC: NASW.

Biggerstaff, M. A. (2000). A critique of the Model State Social Work Practice Act. *Social Work, 45*(2), 105–115.

Black, P. N., & Whelley, J. (1999). The social work licensure exam: Examining the exam through the lens of CSWE curriculum policy. *Arête, 23*, 66–72.

Black-Hughes, C. (December, 2008). Identification of the numbers of persons licensed as social workers serving underserved communities and culturally and ethnically diverse communities. Report to the Minnesota Board of Social Work and Legislature. Available at http://www.socialwork.state.mn.us/.

Bogo, M., & McKnight, K. (2005). Clinical supervision in social work: A review of the research literature. *The Clinical Supervisor, 24*(1–2), 49–67.

Boland-Prom, K. W. (2009). Results from a national study of social workers sanctioned by state licensing boards. *Social Work, 54*(4), 351–360.

Borenzweig, H. (1977). Who passes the California licensing examinations? *Social Work, 22*, 173–177.

Boutté-Queen, N. M. (2003). *Identifying barriers to obtaining social work licensure.* Unpublished doctoral dissertation, University of Houston, Texas.

Boutté-Queen, N. (2009). Profession(al) in environment: Our changing reality. *NASW/Texas Network, 33*(7), 9.

Briggs, L. A., Brown, H., Kesten, K., & Heath, J. (2006). Certification. *Critical Care Nurse, 26*(6), 47–53.

British Association of Social Workers (BASW). (2002). *The code of ethics for social work.* Birmingham, UK: British Association of Social Workers. Available at http://www.basw.co.uk/Portals/0/CODE%20OF%20ETHICS.pdf.

Bruce, E. J., & Austin, M. (2000). Social work supervision: Assessing the past and mapping the future. *The Clinical Supervisor, 19*(2), 85–107.

Buechner, F. (1973). *Wishful thinking: A theological ABC.* New York: Harper and Row.

Bunker, D. R., & Wijnberg, M. H. (1988). *Supervision and performance: Managing professional work in human service organizations.* San Francisco: Jossey-Bass.

Care Standards Act 2000. Available at http://www.opsi.gov.uk/acts/acts2000/en/ukpgaen_20000014_en_e1.

Caspi, J., & Reid, W. J. (2002). *Educational supervision in social work: A task-centered model for field instruction and staff development.* New York: Columbia University Press.

Cavazos, A. (2001). Baccalaureate social work licensure: Its effects on salary and use of job titles. *The Journal of Baccalaureate Social Work, 6*(2), 69–80.

Center for Workforce Studies. (2006). *Assuring sufficiency of a frontline workforce: A national study of licensed social workers.* Washington, DC: NASW.

Cherry, A., Rothman, B., & Skolnik, L. (1989). Licensure as a dilemma for social work education: Findings of a national study. *Journal of Social Work Education, 25*(3), 168–175.

Cloutier, K. G. (1997). *Licensing public social workers in selected states.* Unpublished master's thesis. Augsburg College, Minneapolis, MN.

Cohen, M. B., & Deri, R. (1992). The dilemma of "grandparenting" in state licensure: Confronting the training needs of nondegreed workers. *Social Work, 37*(2), 155–158.

Collins, D., Coleman, H., & Miller, P. (2002). Regulation of social work: A confusing landscape. *Canadian Social Work Review, 19*(2), 205–225.

Corazzini-Gomez, K. (2002). The relative effects of home care client characteristics on the resource allocation process: Do personality and demeanor matter? *The Gerontologist, 42*(6), 740–750.

Council for Healthcare Regulatory Excellence. (2009). *Report and recommendations to the Secretary of State for Health on the conduct function of the General Social Care Council.* London: Author.

Council on Social Work Education (CSWE). (Fall 2001). Council releases position statement on licensing of educators. *Social Work Education Reporter, 49*(3), 3, 8.

Council on Social Work Education (CSWE). (2008). *Educational policy and accreditation standards.* Alexandria, VA: Author.

Cox, D., & Pawar, M. (2006). *International social work: Issues, strategies, and programs.* Thousand Oaks, CA: Sage.

Croninger, R. G., Rice, J. K., Rathbun, A., & Nishio, M. (2007). Teacher qualifications and early learning: Effects of certification, degree, and experience on first-grade achievement. *Economics of Education Review, 26*(3), 312–324.

Daley, M. R., & Doughty, M. O. (2006). Ethics complaints in social work practice: A rural-urban comparison. *Journal of Social Work Values and Ethics, 4*(2). Available at www.socialworker.com/jswve.

Daley, M. R., & Doughty, M. O. (2007). Preparing BSWs for ethical practice: Lessons from licensing data. *Journal of Social Work Values and Ethics, 4*(2). Available at www.socialworker.com/jswve.

DeAngelis, D. (2000). Addressing confusion over state licensing. CSWE *Reporter,* Spring/Summer 2000, Letter to the Editor, p. 9.

DeAngelis, D. (2001). Who is really served by exemptions? *ASWB Association News, 11*(1), 2, 11.

DeAngelis, D., & Monahan, M. J. 2008. Professional credentials and professional regulations: Social work professional development. In B. White (Vol. Ed.), *Comprehensive handbook of social work and social welfare* (Vol. I, pp. 65–74). Hoboken, NJ: Wiley.

Department of Health (DH). (2002) *Requirements for social work training.* London: Department of Health. Available at http://www.dh.gov.uk/en/Publications andstatistics/Publications/PublicationsPolicyAndGuidance/DH_4007803.

Desai, A. (1987). Development of social work education. In *Encyclopedia of Social Work in India,* vol. 2, pp. 221–235. New Delhi: Government of India, Ministry of Welfare.

Desai, M., & Narayan, L. (1998). Challenges for social work profession: Towards people centered development. *The Indian Journal of Social Work, 59*(1), 131–141.

DiNitto, K. M., & McNeece, C. A. (2008). *Social work issues and opportunities in a challenging profession* (3rd ed.). Chicago: Lyceum Books, Inc.

Doelling, C. N. (1997). *Social work career development: A handbook for job hunting and career planning.* Washington, DC: NASW Press.

Dubois, B., & Miley, K. K. (1999). *Social work: An empowering profession* (3rd ed.) Boston: Allyn & Bacon.

Elliott, D., & Mayadas, N. (1999). Infusing global perspectives into social work practice. In C. S. Ramanathan & R. J. Link, *All our futures: Principles and resources for social work practice in a global era* (pp. 52–68). Belmont, CA: Wadsworth Publishing Company.

Epple, D. M. (2007). Inter and intra professional social work difference: Social work's challenge. *Clinical Social Work, 35*(4), 267–276.

Farley, O. W., Smith, L. L., & Boyle, S. W. (2006). *Introduction to social work* (10th ed.). Boston: Pearson Education, Inc.

Federation of Associations of Regulatory Boards. (2001, October). Model application for licensure and renewal. Author, Evanston, IL. Available at www.farb.org.

Freire, P. (1989). *Pedagogy of the oppressed.* New York: Continuum.

Gambrill, E., & Pruger, R. (Eds.). (1992). *Controversial issues in social work.* Boston: Allyn & Bacon.

Gandy, J. T., & Raymond, F. B. (1979). A study of strategies used in the pursuit of legal regulation of social work. *Journal of Sociology and Social Welfare, 6*(4), 464–476.

Garcia, A. (1990a). An examination of the social work profession's efforts to achieve legal regulation. *Journal of Counseling and Development, 68,* 491–497.

Garcia, A. (1990b). Social work and related mental health professions: Toward mutual understanding, legal regulation, and collaboration. *Journal of Counseling and Development, 68,* 505–506.

Gellis, Z. D., McClive-Reed, K., & McCracken, S. G. (2008). Depression in older adults with dementia. In S. Diwan (Ed.), *Mental health and older adults resource review.* CSWE Gero-Ed Center, Master's Advanced Curriculum Project. Retrieved on November 2009, from http://depts.washington.edu/geroctr/mac/1_5mental.html.

General Social Care Council (GSCC). (2004). *Code of Practice for Social Care Workers and Code of Practice for Employers of Social Care Workers.* London: General Social Care Council. Available at http://www.gscc.org.uk/codes.

General Social Care Council (GSCC). 2008. (Conduct) Rules. Available at http://www.gscc.org.uk/NR/rdonlyres/67F9C9D2-DE3E-4287-927C-C987911EB29D/0/2008GSCCConductRules.pdf.

General Social Care Council (GSCC). (2009). Become a social worker. Retrieved April 3, 2009, from http://www.gscc.org.uk.

Glicken, M. D. (2007). *Social work in the 21st century: An introduction to social welfare, social issues, and the profession.* Thousand Oaks, CA: Sage.

Goldsmith, S. A. (1931). Registration of social workers. In *Proceedings of the*

National Conference of Social Work (pp. 551–562). Chicago: University of Chicago Press.

Gray, S. W. (1990). The interplay of social work licensure and supervision: An exploratory study. *The Clinical Supervisor, 8*(1), 53–65.

Grosch, E. N. (2006). Does specialty board certification influence clinical outcomes? *Journal of Evaluation in Clinical Practice, 12*(5), 473–481.

Groshong, L. W. (2009). *Clinical social work practice and regulation: An overview.* Lanham, MD: University Press of America.

Gross, S. J. (1978). The myth of professional licensing. *American Psychologist, 33,* 1009–1016.

Gunavathy, J. S. (2007). India. In I. Weiss & P. Welbourne (Eds.), *Social work as a profession: A comparative cross-national perspective* (pp. 85–104). Birmingham, UK: Venture Press/BASW.

Hakel, M. D., Koenig, J. A., & Elliott, S. W. (Eds.). (2008). *Assessing accomplished teaching: Advanced level teaching certification programs.* Washington, DC: The National Academies Press. Summary retrieved on September 25, 2008, from http://www.nationalacademies.org/.

Hardcastle, D. A. (1977). Public regulation of social work. *Social Work, 22*(1), 14–20.

Hare, I. (2004). Defining social work for the 21st century: The International Federation of Social Workers' revised definition of social work. *International Social Work, 47*(3), 407–424.

Hasenfeld, Y. (2010). Worker-client relations: Social policy in practice. In Y. Hasenfeld, *Human services as complex organizations* (2nd ed.) (pp. 405–425). Thousand Oaks, CA: Sage.

Haydn Jones, H. (1994). *Social workers, or social educators? The international context for developing social care.* London: National Institute for Social Work.

Healy, L. M. (2001). *International social work: Professional action in an independent world.* New York: Oxford University Press.

Healy, L. M., & Hokenstad, T. M. C. (2008). International social work. In T. Mizrahi & L. E. Davis, *Encyclopedia of social work* (pp. 482–493). Washington, DC: NASW and Oxford University Press.

Healy, L. M., & Link, R. J. (Eds.). (Forthcoming). *Handbook on international social work and human rights.* New York: Oxford University P

Herrick, J. M., & Stuart, P. H. (Eds.). (2005). *Encyclopedia of social welfare history.* Thousand Oaks, CA: Sage.

Hickman, S. (1994). Social work licensing. *ACSW Journal, 1*(1), 133–141.

Hokenstad, M. C., Khinduka, S. K., & Midgley, J. (Eds.). (1992). *Profiles in international social work.* Washington, DC: NASW.

Hoffman, K. (2002). The basics of social work licensing. *The New Social Worker, 9*(2), 28–30.

Holcomb, R. (2002). Social work licensure: Reviewing the controversy. In P. Luinenburg, K. Zacher-Pate, R. Holcomb, & A. A. Bibus, *Choices and responsibilities for social workers: Licensure and the professional associations* (pp. 26–29). Minneapolis, MN: Minnesota Board of Social Work and Minnesota Coalition of Licensed Social Workers.

Holcomb, R. (2003). Universal licensure. Public agency social worker attitudes. Unpublished paper, University of St. Thomas, St. Paul, MN.

Hollings, R. L., & Pike-Nase, C. (1997). *Professional and occupational licensure in the United States: An annotated bibliography and professional resource.* Westport, CT: Greenwood Press.

Ife, J. (2001). *Human rights and social work: Towards rights based practice.* Cambridge: Cambridge University Press.

International Association of Schools of Social Work (IASSW). (2004). Global standards for the education and training of the social work profession. Available at www.iassw-aietz.org.

International Federation of Social Workers (IFSW). (2005). International policy statement on globalization and the environment (adopted October 25, 2005). Bern, Switzerland: Author.

International Federation of Social Workers (IFSW). (2009). Social worker to be accredited in Singapore. Available at http://www.ifsw.org/p38001788.html.

International Federation of Social Workers (IFSW), & International Association of Schools of Social Work (IASSW). (2004). Ethics in social work, Statement of principles. Bern, Switzerland: Author.

Johnson, D. A., & Huff, D. (1987). Licensing exams: How valid are they? *Social Work, 32*(2), 159–161.

Johnson, D. A., & Huff, D. (1989). Testing: How important is it to licensing for social work practice? *Journal of Independent Social Work, 3*(2), 9–21.

Jost, T. S. (Ed.). *Regulation of the healthcare professions.* (1997). Chicago: Health Administration Press.

Kadushin, A., & Harkness, D. (2002). *Supervision in social work* (4th ed.). New York: Columbia University Press.

Kaiser, T. L. (1997). *Supervisory relationships: Exploring the human element.* Pacific Grove, CA: Brooks/Cole.

Karger, H. J. (1988). Unions and social work licensure. In H. J. Karger (Ed.), *Social workers and labor unions* (pp. 37–46). Westport, CT: Greenwood Press.

Karls, J. M. (1992). Should social workers be licensed? Yes. In E. Gambrill & R. Pruger (Eds.), *Controversial issues in social work* (pp. 53–57). Boston: Allyn & Bacon.

Khinduka, S. K. (2008). Globalization. In T. Mizrahi & L. E. Davis, *Encyclopedia of social work* (Vol. 2, pp. 275–279). Washington, DC: NASW and Oxford University Press.

Kinderknecht, C. (1995). *Social work ethical violations: The experience of one state regulatory board.* Unpublished doctoral dissertation, University of Kansas.

Kleiner, M. M. (2006). *Licensing occupations: Ensuring quality or restricting competition?* Kalamazoo, MI: W. E. Upjohn Institute for Employment Research.

Kondrat, M. E. (2008). Person-in-environment. In T. Mizrahi & L. E. Davis (Eds.), *Encyclopedia of social work* (Vol. 3, pp. 348–353). Washington, DC: Oxford University Press and NASW.

Konopka, G. (1958). *Eduard C. Lindeman and social work philosophy.* Minneapolis, MN: The University of Minnesota Press.

Ladd, H. F., Sass, T. R., & Harris, D. N. (2007). The impact of national board certified teachers on student achievement in Florida and North Carolina: A summary of the evidence prepared for the National Academies Committee on Evaluation of the Impact of Teacher Certification by NBPTS. Retrieved on September 25, 2008, from http://www.nationalacademies.org/.

Land, H. (1988). The impact of licensing on social work practice: Values, ethics, choices. *Journal of Independent Social Work, 2*(4), 87–96.

Lavalette, M., & Ferguson, I. (Eds.). *International social work and the radical tradition.* (2007). Birmingham, UK: Venture Press.

Law, M. T., & Kim, S. (2005). Specialization and regulation: The rise of professionals and the emergence of occupational licensing regulation. *Journal of Economic History, 65*(3), 723–756.

Lieberman, A. A., Shatkin, B. F., & McGuire, T. G. (1988). Assessing the effect of vendorship: A one-state case study. *Journal of Independent Social Work, 2*(4), 59–74.

Liles, R. E. (2008). Response to "Licensing social work faculty: An issue of ethics?" A response to the editorial comment: Licensing of social work faculty in the *Journal of Social Work Values and Ethics, 3*(2). Available at www.socialworker.com/jswve. Retrieved October 31, 2008.

Link, R. J., & Bibus, A. A. (2000). *When children pay: US welfare reform and its implications for UK policy.* London: Child Poverty Action Group.

Link, R. J., & Healy, L. M. (Eds.). (2005). *Teaching international content: Curriculum resources for social work education.* Alexandria, VA: CSWE.

Lorenz, W. (1994). *Social work in a changing Europe.* London: Routledge.

Luinenburg, P. (February 2005). *Removing the licensure exemption for public agency social workers: looking back, looking forward.* St. Paul, MN: Minnesota Coalition of Licensed Social Workers.

Luinenburg, P., Zacher-Pate, K., Holcomb, R., Bibus, A. A. (2002). *Choices and responsibilities for social workers: Licensure and the professional associations.* (A curriculum module for CSWE-accredited bachelor and master's level social work programs in Minnesota, student manual.) Minneapolis, MN: Minnesota Board of Social Work and Minnesota Coalition of Licensed Social Workers.

Lyons, K., Manion, K., & Carlsen, M. (2006). *International perspectives on social work: Global conditions and local practice.* New York: Palgrave Macmillan.

Madden, R. G. (2007). Liability and safety issues in human services management. In J. Aldgate, L. Healy, B. Malcolm, B. Pine, W. Rose, & J. Seden (Eds.), *Enhancing social work management* (pp. 149–177). London: Kingsley Publishers.

Majumdar, A. M. (1965). *Social welfare in India: Mahatma Gandhi's contributions.* New Delhi: Asia Publishing House.

Marson, S. (2006). Editorial comment: Licensing of social work faculty. *Journal of Social Work Values and Ethics, 3*(2). Retrieved October 31, 2008, from www.socialworker.com/jswve.

Marson, S. M., DeAngelis, D., & Mittal, N. (2010). Association of Social Work Board's licensure examinations: A review of reliability and validity processes. *Research on Social Work Practice, 20*(1), 87–99.

Mathis, T. P. (1992). Should social workers be licensed? No. In E. Gambrill & R. Pruger (Eds.), *Controversial issues in social work* (pp. 58–64.). Boston: Allyn & Bacon.

Matz, B. C. (1996). *Allies, adversaries or just apathy? Social work licensure and faculty knowledge and perceptions.* Unpublished doctoral dissertation, West Virginia University, Morgantown, WV.

Mayadas, N. S., Watts, T. D., & Elliot, D. (Eds.). (1997). *International handbook on social work theory and practice.* Westport, CT: Greenwood Press.

McCann, C. W., & Cutler, J. P. (1979). Ethics and the alleged unethical. *Social Work, 24,* 5–8.

McCarthy, J. (2008). Licensure: *The good, the bad and the unknown.* Unpublished doctoral dissertation, Sarah Lawrence College, Bronxville, NY.

MedHunters. (2009). Licensing: Social workers—Canada. Retrieved April 3, 2009, from http://www.medhunters.com/articles/licensingSocialWorkCanada.html#CanLicensing.

Middleman, R. R. (1984). How competent is social work's approach to the assessment of competence? *Social Work, 29*(2), 146–153.

Midgley, J. (1997). *Social welfare in a global context.* Thousand Oaks, CA: Sage.

Minnesota Association of County Social Service Administrators. (2003). 2003 legislative position: Requiring licensure of all county social workers by the state Board of Social Work. St. Paul, MN: Author.

Minnesota Board of Nursing. (March 27, 2009). Findings of Fact, Conclusion and Final Order in the matter of William Melchret-Denkel, L. P. N.

Minnesota Board of Social Work. (2008). *Biennial report: 2006–2008.* Minneapolis, MN: Author.

Minnesota Department of Human Services. (2007). *Baseline of competency: Common licensing standards for mental health professionals.* St. Paul, MN: Author's report to the state legislature, January 15, 2007. Available at http://www.socialwork.state.mn.us/.

Mizrahi, T., & Davis, L. E. (Eds.). (2008). *The encyclopedia of social work* (20th ed.). New York, Oxford: Oxford University Press.

Morales, A. T., & Sheafor, B. W. (2001). *Social work: A profession of many faces* (9th ed.). Boston: Allyn & Bacon.

Munson, C. E. (2002). *Clinical social work supervision* (3rd ed.). New York: Hayworth Press.

Nagpaul, H. (2005). *Social work in urban India.* Jaipur: Rawat Publications.

Nanavatty, M. C. (1997). India. In N. S. Mayadas, T. D. Watts, & D. Elliot (Eds.), *International handbook on social work theory and practice* (pp. 245–262). Westport, CT: Greenwood Press.

National Association of Social Workers (NASW). (June, 2005). Social work licensure: Practice and title protection reviewed. Retrieved, June 2005, from www.socialworkers.org/ldf/leg.

National Association of Social Workers (NASW). (2007). From NASW's paper comparing the code of ethics and state licensing laws. Available at http://www.socialworkers.org/ldf/legal_issue/200706.asp.

National Association of Social Workers (NASW). (2008). *Code of ethics.* Washington, DC: Author. Available at www.socialworkers.org.

National Association of Social Workers (NASW). (2009). *National Association of Social Workers policy statements.* Washington, DC: Author.

National Association of Social Workers & Association of Social Work Boards (NASW/ASWB). (2005). *Standards for technology and social work practice.* Washington, DC: Authors. NASW's Legal Issues of the Month (April 17, 2009).

National Conference of Social Work. (1931). *Proceedings of the National Conference of Social Work, Minneapolis, June 14–20, 1931.* Chicago: University of Chicago Press.

"Now about the little guy . . . ." (2007, December). This article featured Roger Kryzanek, the outgoing president of the Association of Social Work Boards. *ASWB Association News, 17*(6), 1, 11.

Overson, C. (2005). *Universal licensure exemption: Minnesota social service employees respond.* Unpublished master's clinical paper, College of St. Catherine/University of St. Thomas School of Social Work, St. Paul, MN.

Pardeck, J. T., Chung, W. S, & Murphy, J. W. (1997). Degreed and nondegreed licensed clinical social workers: An exploratory study. *Journal of Sociology and Social Welfare, 24*(2), 143–158.

Payne, M. (2007a). *What is professional social work?* (2nd ed.). Chicago: Lyceum Books, Inc.

Payne, M. (2007b). United Kingdom. In I. Weiss & P. Welbourne (Eds.), *Social work as a profession: A comparative cross-national perspective* (pp. 179–203). Birmingham, UK: Venture Press.

Payne, M., & Askeland, G. A. (2008). *Globalization and international social work: Postmodern change and challenge.* Aldershot, UK: Ashgate.

Payne, M., & Shardlow, S. (2002). *Social work in the British Isles.* London: Jessica Kingsley.

Pew Commission for the 21st Century. (December, 1995). *Reforming health care workforce regulation: Report of the Task Force on Health Care Workforce Regulation.* San Francisco: Author.

Poertner, J. (2006). Social administration and outcomes for consumers: What do we know? *Administration in Social Work, 30*(2), 11–24.

Quality Assurance Agency (QAA). (2008). *Social work.* Mansfield, UK: The Quality Assurance Agency for Higher Education. Available at http://www.qaa.ac.uk/academicinfrastructure/benchmark/statements/ socialwork08.pdf.

Ramanathan, C. S., & Link, R. J. (1999). *All our futures: Principles and resources for social work practice in a global era.* Belmont, CA: Wadsworth Publishing Company.

Randall, A. D., & DeAngelis, D. (2008). Licensing. In T. Mizrahi & L. E. Davis,

Editors-in-Chief, *Encyclopedia of social work* (Vol. 3, pp. 87–91). New York: NASW and Oxford University Press.

Randall, E. J., & Thyer, B. A. (1994). A preliminary test of the validity of the LCSW examination. *Clinical Social Work Journal, 22*(2), 223–227.

Reaves, R. P. (2006). The history of licensure of psychologists in the United States and Canada. In T. J. Vaughn (Ed.), *Psychology licensing and certification* (pp. 17–26). Washington, DC: American Psychological Association.

Reichert, E. (2003). *Social work and human rights: A foundation for policy and practice.* New York: Columbia University Press.

Reisch, M., & Andrews, J. (2002). *The road not taken: A history of radical social work in the United States.* New York: Brunner-Routledge.

Robb, M. (2004). Chaos theory: Hope for licensure reform in the post-9/11 age? *Social Work Today, 4*(5), 17–21.

Ronan, T., & Freeman, A. (2007). *Cognitive behavior therapy in clinical social work practice.* New York: Springer Publishing.

Rooney, R. H. (2009). *Strategies for work with involuntary clients* (2nd ed.). New York: Columbia University Press.

Rouse, W. A. (2008). National Board certified teachers are making a difference in student achievements: Myth or fact? *Leadership and Policy in Schools, 7,* 64–86.

Saltzman, A., & Proch, K. (1990). *Law in social work practice.* Chicago: Nelson-Hall.

Scheyett, A., Kim, M., Swanson, J., Swartz, M., Elbogen, E., Van Dorn, R., et al. (2009). Autonomy and the use of directive intervention in the treatment of individuals with serious mental illnesses: A survey of social work practitioners. *Social Work in Mental Health, 7*(4), 283–306.

Schock, M. D., & Bosch, L. A. (In press). Local capacity building in humanitarian crises. In N. T. Tan (Ed.), *Community and strengths perspectives in disaster management and recovery.* New York: Routledge Press.

Schriver J. M. (2001). *Human behavior and the social environment: Shifting paradigms in essential knowledge for social work practice* (3rd ed.). Needham Heights, MA: Allyn & Bacon.

Schroeder, L. O. (1995). *The legal environment of social work.* Washington, DC: NASW.

Schwartz, S., & Dattalo, P. (1990). Factors affecting student selection of macro specializations. *Administration in Social Work, 14*(3), 83–96.

Segal, E. A., & Brzuzy, S. (1998). *Social welfare policy, programs, and practice.* Itasca, IL: F. E. Peacock Publishers.

Seidl, F. W. (2000). Should licensure be required for faculty who teach direct practice courses? No! *Journal of Social Work Education, 36*(2), 193–200.

Sfiligoj, H. (2009). States struggle with varying regulations: Licensure protects public, raises issues for social workers. *NASW News, 54*(2), 9.

Shardlow, S., & Payne, M. (Eds.). (1998). *Contemporary issues in social work: Western Europe.* Aldershot, UK: Ashgate.

Shimberg, B. (1985). Overview of professional and occupational licensing. In J. C.

Fortune (Ed.), *Understanding testing in occupational licensing: Establishing links between principles of measurement and practices in licensing* (pp. 1–14). San Francisco: Jossey-Bass.

Shulman, L. (1993). *Interactional supervision.* Washington, DC: NASW.

Shulman, L. (2008). Supervision. In T. Mizrahi & L. E. Davis (Eds.), *Encyclopedia of social work* (Vol. 4, pp. 186–190). Washington, DC: NASW/Oxford University Press.

Simons, K. V. (2006). Organizational characteristics influencing nursing home social service directors' qualifications: A national study. *Health & Social Work, 31*(4), 266–274.

Strom-Gottfried, K. (2000). Ensuring ethical practice: An examination of NASW Code violations. *Social Work, 45*(3), 251–261.

Strom-Gottfried, K. (2003). Understanding adjudication: Origins, targets and outcomes of ethics complaints. *Social Work, 48*(1), 85–94.

Surface, D. (2009). Understanding evidence-based practice in behavioral health. *Social Work Today, 9*(4), 22–25.

Sutherland, K., & Leatherman, S. (2008). Does certification improve medical standards? *British Medical Journal, 333*(7565), 439–441.

Tamblyn, R., Abrahamowicz, M., Dauphinee, W. D., Henley, J., Norcini, J., Girard, et al. (2002). Association between licensure examination scores and practice in primary care. *Journal of the American Medical Association, 288*(23), 3019–3026.

Tan, N. T., & Rowlands, A. (Eds.). (2004). *Social work around the world: III.* Bern, Switzerland: International Federation of Social Workers.

Tan, N. T. & Rowlands, A. (2008). Social redevelopment following the Indian Ocean tsunami. *Social Development Issues, 30*(1), 47–58.

Tan, T. (2009). Disaster management: Strengths and community perspectives. *Journal of Global Social Work Practice.* Available at http://www.globalsocialwork. org/vol2no1_Tan.html.

Teasley, M. L., Baffour, T. D., & Tyson, E. H. (2005). Perceptions of cultural competence among urban school social workers: Does experience make a difference? *Children & Schools, 27*(4), 227–237.

Texas State Board of Social Work Examiners. (2009). Alternative method of examining competency. Retrieved September 19, 2009, from www.dshs.state. tx.us/SocialWork/lsw_amec.doc.

Thungjaroenkul, P., Cummings, G. G., & Embleton, A. (2007). The impact of nurse staffing on hospital costs and patient length of stay: A systematic review. *Nursing Economics, 25*(5), 255–265.

Thyer, B. A. (1994). Assessing competence for social work practice: The role of standardized tests. In R. G. Meinert, J. T. Pardeck, & W. P. Sullivan (Eds.), *Issues in social work: A critical analysis* (pp. 67–81). Westport, CT: Greenwood Press.

Thyer, B. A. (2000). Should licensure be required for faculty who teach direct practice courses? Yes! *Journal of Social Work Education, 36*(2), 187–192.

Thyer, B. A. (2010). LCSW examination pass rates: Implications for social work education. *Clinical Social Work Journal,* online publication. Available at http://springerlink.com/content/j482361260273362/ ?p = 4a9baf46364643eea5ef5dea3bd6eaae&pi = 8.

Thyer, B. A., & Biggerstaff, M. A. (1989). *Professional social work credentialing and legal regulation.* Springfield, IL: Thomas.

Thyer, B. A., & Vodde, R. (1994). Is the ACSW examination valid? *Clinical Social Work Journal, 22*(1), 105–112.

TOPSS UK Partnership (2002) *The National Occupational Standards for Social Work.* Leeds: Skills for Care. Available at http://www.york.ac.uk/depts/spsw/documents/3SWNOSdocpdffileseditionApro4.pdf.

Tracy, M. B. (1992). Cross-national social welfare policy analysis in the graduate curriculum: A comparative process model. *Journal of Social Work Education, 28*(3), 341–352.

Trattner, W. I. (1999). *From Poor Law to welfare state: A history of social welfare in America* (6th ed.). New York: Free Press.

Trotter, C. (1999). *Working with involuntary clients.* Sydney, Australia: Allen and Unwin.

Tsui, M-S. (2005). *Social work supervision: Contexts and concepts.* Thousand Oaks, CA: Sage.

Turner, F. (1997). Canada. In N. S. Mayadas, T. D. Watts, & D. Elliot (Eds.), *International handbook on social work theory and practice* (pp. 29–48). Westport, CT: Greenwood Press.

Van Wormer, K. (1997). *Social welfare: A world view.* Chicago: Nelson Hall.

Vaughn, H. T., Rogers, J. L., Freeman, J. K. (2006). Does requiring continuing education units for professional licensing renewal assure quality patient care? *The Health Care Manager, 25*(1), 78–84.

Viadero, D, & Honawar, V. (2008). Credential of NBPTS has impact: Still, evidence is scant that program transformed field. *Education Week, 27*(42), 1–2.

Walker, J. S, Briggs, H. E., Koroloff, N., & Friesen, B. J. (2007). Implementing and sustaining evidence-based practice in social work. *Journal of Social Work Education, 43*(3), 361–375.

Walley, P. (2007). Alabama's comprehensive child welfare system reform. *Policy & Practice, 65*(1), 18–20.

Walsh, P. (October 15, 2009). Nurse involved in suicide chats loses license. *Star Tribune, 28*(194), A1, A8.

Weinbach, R. W. (2005). *Evaluating social work services and programs.* Boston: Allyn & Bacon.

Weiss, I., Gal, J., & Dixon, J. (Eds.). (2003). *Professional ideologies and preferences in social work: A global study.* Westport, CT: Praeger.

Weiss, I., & Welbourne, P. (Eds.). (2007). *Social work as a profession: A comparative cross-national perspective.* Birmingham, UK: Venture Press/BASW.

Whitaker, T. (2009). *The results are in: What social workers say about social work.* Washington, DC: NASW.

Whitaker, T., Weismiller, T., & Clark, E. (2006). *Assuring the sufficiency of a front-line workforce: A national study of licensed social workers.* Washington, DC: National Association of Social Workers.

Zárate, Z. G. J., & Treviño, G. G. (2007). Mexico. In I. Weiss & P. Welbourne (Eds.), *Social work as a profession: A comparative cross-national perspective* (pp. 105–118). Birmingham, UK: Venture Press/BASW.

Suggested Learning Activities and Discussion Questions

1. Turn to the table of contents and index of your introductory text-book and search for terms related to regulation (regulation, certi-fication, licensure). Note how often each is referenced, how each is defined (if at all), and see whether the information provided is broad or specific.

2. Interview your professors or field instructors about licensing. Are they licensed? Why or why not?

3. Using the LICENSEE framework, analyze the social work regula-tory policies in your state or jurisdiction. Try both the table and narrative formats.

4. Conduct a search for studies in your region examining the impact of social work regulations on the quality of client services. In addition to searching databases, be sure to contact your local board for reports and strategic plans. What are some of the fac-tors that promote or discourage studies into the effects of licens-ing social workers? What would you recommend be done to increase, expand, or more usefully focus such research?

5. Ask someone who has used social work services (e.g., your practi-cum agency's clients) to share insights about licensure. Do clients typically know or care if their social worker is licensed? What has been the impact (if any) that licensing of social workers has had on clients' lives?

6. Interview a colleague from another country concerning the role of regulation of social work there. Are professions licensed or regulated in another way? Is social work licensed?

7. Compare the definitions of social work established by the various nations featured in chapter 3. What similarities and differences

do you note between them and in comparison with the definition of social work in your state's regulations?

8. What emerging issues or controversies related to licensing in addition to the ones discussed in chapter 4 can you identify? For example, what are the implications of the attempt to secure universal health-care coverage in the United States? Will the constrictions in services available that emerged out of managed care continue, or will there be a renewed expansion of more universal social services as a critical dimension of health care?

9. What are the impacts of the global economic crises and the credit freeze on social work licensees, many of whom have large student loans and face increasing fees related to obtaining and maintaining their license?

10. Identify at least three challenges to social work licensure faced by yourself or your peers. What are they? What are potential opportunities for overcoming those barriers?

11. Discuss the role of professional associations compared to the role of regulatory boards. Do you plan to maintain membership in NASW or other professional associations in addition to maintaining your license? Why or why not?

12. Develop a proposal for a grant to fund research evaluating the outcomes of social work licensure in your jurisdiction.

13. Look at the ASWB Table of Exam Committee Composition, 1999–2009 (table 4.1). Given your understanding of the purpose of the examination committee (see ASWB's website), identify at least three strengths in the composition of the committee over the past ten years and at least three areas of difficulty.

14. Explore the resources listed in appendix B. For example, can you find other grassroots advocacy groups such as the National Alliance on Mental Health that may have an interest in working for improvements in social work licensure in your area? Consider developing a project to submit to the Influencing State Policy annual contest. Or write an article on licensing in your state to submit to your local NASW chapter's newsletter or another journal.

Annotated List of Selected Resources

This appendix offers an annotated list of selected resources for students to consider in understanding, evaluating, and tapping the benefits of licensing for fostering professional development and client services and for influencing regulations and regulators. The list is not intended to be exhaustive; rather, items are representative of other similar resources. Readers are encouraged to explore these and to send to the authors suggestions for resources to add in subsequent editions of this primer: care of Lyceum Books, Inc.

Association for the Advancement of Social Work with Groups (AASWG)

http://www.aaswg.org/
This international professional organization was founded in 1979 to "promote excellence in group work practice, education, field instruction, research and publication." The association has some local chapters in North America and Germany, and hosts an annual international symposium that is inclusive and wide-ranging in workshops and events of interest to students. Its newly revamped website is easy to navigate. Its global group work network provides opportunities for members to compare notes on what elements of group practice are shared across countries and cultures and what elements are specialized to a particular culture or locale. Of particular interest with regard to regulation of social work, AASWG has published a set of *Standards for Social Work Practice with Groups*, available through its website.

Association of Baccalaureate Program Directors (BPD)

http://www.bpdonline.org
This professional association of social work educators involved in undergraduate programs began with a conference organized by BSW program directors in the early 1970s. While still offering an excellent annual conference, it has expanded membership to include social work faculty and provides a number of other resources and supports for social work educators and students. Its website is handy, and its electronic mailing list discussion forum, BPD List, is a mainstay for members' discussions, resource sharing, and timely advice and guidance. The association has adopted an influential definition of generalist practice; prominent in its strategic plan under the first goal to promote leadership in BSW education is "Objective 2: Advocate for and promote baccalaureate social work generalist practice, [with its] Task 2: Establish the CSWE accredited BSW degree as the foundation for professional social work practice (Advocacy Committee) and OUTCOME: Lobby for state licensure of BSW graduates."

Association of Community Organization, Supervision, and Administration (ACOSA)

http://www.acosa.org/
Members of this professional association include social workers, supervisors, educators, administrators, community organizers, students, and others interested in advocating, networking, and researching on behalf of community organization and social administration. Through its annual symposium, publications, awards, and other shared resources, it is an informative and active source of support and information for efforts to influence organizations and policies at a macro level, such as those related to regulating practice. It is also one of the national associations where supervisors can find mutual aid and shared interests.

Association of Social Work Boards (ASWB; formerly American Association of State Social Work Boards)

http://www.aswb.org/
ASWB is the premier source of information about social work regulation in Canada and the United States. It is established and governed by the boards that regulate social work in both countries. Originally, its primary purpose was to develop a standardized examination to test whether candidates had the minimum competencies for licensure. Since 1978, it has gradually expanded its services to member boards and now offers orientation

and training to board members and staff, annual meetings and conferences, a program for approving continuing education providers (ACE), a registry for licensees to centralize information on their credentials, the Disciplinary Action Reporting System (DARS) for collecting records on licensing violations, a model act to guide jurisdictions' licensing statutes, and other services (including managing one state's application process). Social work licensing examinations still are the main product of the association, and fees for the examination support the association's work. Its website is packed with information and has been the major resource for this primer. In addition to online registration for the examination and other test-related resources and products (such as an online practice test), the website has links to ASWB products and resources, newsletters, member services, and other associations. Its search feature is set up for using Google to search the ASWB site as well as generally.

Canadian Association of Social Workers

http://www.casw-acts.ca/
This association's members are nine provincial and one territorial social work organizations in Canada. It was founded in 1926 and works to represent social workers at an international as well as national level. Its mission statement is on the association's website: "CASW is the voice of social workers in Canada promoting excellence in social work practice, education and research and supporting provincial/territorial regulation in the interest of a just and sustainable society."

As one of its three strategic directions, the association is focusing efforts and resources on enhancing excellence in regulation of social work; its website links to authoritative resources regarding registration of social work practitioners. It is a very useful starting point for students interested in internship or employment opportunities in Canada. It has developed a code of ethics (available on its website). Among its publications is its peer-reviewed professional journal *Canadian Social Work*.

Clinical Social Work Association (CSWA)

http://www.clinicalsocialworkassociation.org
This is a national association of clinical social workers with several affiliated societies of clinical social workers at the state level. It provides support, services, and resources to its members and has developed a code of ethics that is available on the association's easily navigated website. Other resources are useful for studies related to the status of the profession of

social work and regulation of practice, including the recently published book *Clinical Social Work Practice and Regulation* by Laura W. Groshong (see the reference list).

Clinical Supervision

In addition to references cited in chapter 4, two sets of supervision standards could be useful for licensing supervisors and regulators as well as licensees. One is the U.S. Children's Bureau's tools on ethics and supervision, including manuals on supervising child protection social workers, published in 2004 and available through the Child Welfare Information Gateway at http://www.childwelfare.gov/systemwide/ethical/supervision_ethics.cfm.

Another licensing supervision resource is the Position Statement on Clinical Supervision from the American Board of Examiners in Clinical Social Work, part of the Center for Clinical Social Work: http://www.abecsw.org/pub-position-papers.html.

Although not readily searchable, the center's website has links to the center's resources and other organizations: http://www.centercsw.org/home.html.

The links to the uniformed services and the federal veteran's services may be of particular interest; social workers need only be licensed in one state to practice anywhere as a social worker for the U.S. Department of Veteran Affairs. The center also provides support and advocacy for clinical social workers, including a code of ethics and model practice act.

See also NASW's and ASWB's websites for more information and training resources in licensing supervision.

Council on Licensure, Enforcement and Regulation (CLEAR)

http://www.clearhq.org

This organization is an international association whose members are officials representing various government or publicly legislated boards and regulatory or certifying bodies. It has been in operation for about thirty years and provides educational opportunities to regulators of a wide variety of occupations and professions, including social work. Hosting meetings, conferences, trainings, webinars, and providing consultation on request of members, it focuses on balanced exploration of issues related to credentialing, licensing, examinations, compliance and discipline, regulatory administration, and legislative or policy matters. Public (nonprofessional) members of social work boards have found CLEAR to be a welcoming resource for sharing and contact with others in similar positions on boards regulating professionals and for advocating on behalf of public protection and client rights. Its various publications and website also are useful resources. For example, it has produced a series of analyses of the regulatory models in Canada, Mexico, and the United Kingdom using the same framework of questions so that students can easily compare the approaches to regulation in each country. Also available on the website is an informative sheet of resources for U.S. students interested in practicing in other countries. The website has headlines on regulation news from around the world crawling across the top, and its search feature is excellent.

Council on Social Work Education (CSWE)

http://www.cswe.org/
CSWE's website is a handy resource for up-to-date policies, data, information, and guidance related to accreditation of social work educational programs. For example, students can access the most recent set of educational policy and accreditation standards for which their programs are accountable. There are links to sections on membership, accreditation, scholarships and fellowships, association meetings and conferences, career and professional services, research, publications, centers, institutes, and other resources. A link labeled "FAQ" (Frequently Asked Questions) brings up a set of "Student Questions," one of which relates to licensing and links to ASWB's website: www.aswb.org.

Where Can I Find Information on Licensing?

The Association of Social Work Boards (ASWB) is the association of boards that regulate social work. ASWB develops and maintains the social work licensing examination used across the country, and is a central resource for information on the legal regulation of social work. Through the association, social work boards can share information and work together. ASWB also is available to help individual social workers and social work students with questions they may have about licensing and the social work examinations.

Searching this site is relatively easy. If one enters a term that is not recognized, other suggested search terms appear. CSWE's Gero-Ed Center with its informative website promotes the social work competencies and standards of practice required for work with older people.

Federation of Associations of Regulatory Boards (FARB)

http://www.farb.org

Founded in 1974, this nonprofit organization is, in the words of its website, "an association of associations." Its members include the associations of boards that regulate professionals such as accountants, barbers, cosmetologists, dentists, engineers, long-term care administrators, nurses, occupational therapists, optometrists, pharmacists, physical therapists, psychologists, veterinarians, and social workers. It hosts an annual conference and provides other training opportunities, especially for attorneys who represent regulatory boards. Among its useful published resources are a generic model act, a model code of conduct for board members, and a model application form for licensure and renewal; these models are available to the public for $50 each. Its website has basic features but not a search option; members can log in for other uses and can obtain the models at no cost.

Influencing State Policy

http://www.statepolicy.org/

In March of 1997 at the Annual Program Meeting of the Council on Social Work Education (CSWE) in Chicago, Prof. Bob Schneider from Virginia Commonwealth University invited representatives from the professional associations and any other interested social work educators to a meeting to discuss a proactive, constructive response to the passage of the historic welfare reform bill that had been signed by President Clinton the previous summer: The Personal Responsibility and Work Opportunity Reconciliation Act of 1996. With this repeal of Aid to Families with Dependent Children (AFDC), responsibility for financial assistance to poor families was significantly devolved from the federal government to the states. The group decided to form a national committee to assist faculty and students in learning how to effectively influence social policies at the state level. Over subsequent years, a useful website was developed, instructional videos were produced, a regular newsletter was published, a network of liaisons to social work programs across the country was established, and an annual contest was sponsored resulting in cash awards and recognition at CSWE conferences of student and faculty projects. Contest entries are projects influencing or advocating for a state social policy or a piece of state legislation, so those related to social work regulation would be eligible.

International Association of Schools of Social Work (IASSW)

http://www.iassw-aiets.org

This worldwide association of social work educational institutions has been in existence for more than eighty years. Its website is well organized, and documents such as the Global Standards of Social Work, Definition of Social Work, and an international statement of principles for Ethics in Social Work are easily retrieved. A special feature of its website is its availability in several languages, including Spanish, Arabic, and Japanese. Like IFSW, it serves as a consultant to the United Nations and has members on several U.N. committees; it celebrates the annual Social Work Day at the U.N. with IFSW. With IFSW and the International Conference on Social Welfare, it hosts a biennial international congress for social workers and social work educators, and, with IFSW, it publishes the journal *International Social Work*. There are also regional conferences and gatherings sponsored by IASSW. The association encourages student participation and allots grants of $4,000 each to fund research projects that promise to advance social work internationally. (This grant could be a resource to support research into social work regulation; for example, one recent project was "An Exploratory Study to Identify Some of the Issues Associated with International Migration and Employment of Social Workers."

Contact person: Sue Lawrence: s.lawrence@londonmet.ac.uk).

International Federation of Social Workers (IFSW)

http://www.ifsw.org

This association of social workers from around the world traces its origins to the International Permanent Secretariat of Social Workers (1928) and has operated under its current name with international membership since 1956. According to its annual report, it enjoys membership from eighty nations representing about half a million social workers. Its website is easy to navigate and relatively up-to-date with a wide variety of links to useful resources. For example, as a special consultant to the United Nations Economic and Social Council, IFSW cultivates partnerships with several international organizations (such as Amnesty International) and includes links to them on the website. There is a link to organizations offering volunteer opportunities as well. IFSW participates in hosting international conferences and sponsors the annual World Social Work Day; its newsletter and publications are very useful resources; and, as noted in this primer, its work with IASSW on establishing a global definition of social work, global ethical principles, and global standards for social work practice has been a significant contribution. Global Social Work Standards and other statements related to social work regulation are available as downloadable documents on its website. Among the activities to which the association devotes attention is the promotion of the profession for the purpose of educating social workers, organizations, and the public about the profession; to this end, it has established awards, scholarships, memorial lectures, and a photography contest. With IASSW, it also publishes the journal *International Social Work.*

International Resources

There are now a fair number of good basic resource texts available on international social work. The following citations are selected resources listed in the references: (Cox & Pawar, 2006; Healy, 2001; Healy & Hokenstad, 2008; Healy & Link, forthcoming; Hokenstad, Khinduka, & Midgley, 1992; Ife, 2001; Khinduka, 2008; Lavalette & Ferguson, 2007; Link & Healy, 2005; Lyons, Manion, & Carlsen, 2006; Mayadas, Watts, & Elliott, 1997; Midgley, 1997; Payne, 2007b; Payne & Askeland, 2008; Ramanathan & Link, 1999; Reichert, 2003; Tan & Rowlands, 2004; Van Wormer, 1997; Weiss, Gal, & Dixon, 2003; Weiss & Welbourne, 2007.)

Malcolm Payne's book, written with his Norwegian colleague, Gurid Aga Askeland, is a recent example: Payne, M., & Askeland, G. A. (2008). *Globalization and international social work: Postmodern change and challenge.* Aldershot, UK: Ashgate. The authors argue that social workers have a duty to develop and communicate knowledge, skills, and values in a way that enables people from other cultures to indigenize them within their cultures, and to look for and reinterpret ideas from minority cultures into majority cultures. They expound the practice of cultural translation as a way of transferring understanding between different cultures, and discuss how to handle cross-national practice, such as international placements. Earlier versions of parts of the book were published as articles:

Askeland, G. A., & Payne, M. (2007). Distance education and international social work education. *European Journal of Social Work, 10*(2), 161–174.

Askeland, G., & Payne, M. (2006). Social work education's cultural hegemony. *International Social Work, 49*(4), 731–743.

Askeland, G. A., & Payne, M. (2006). The postmodern student: Piloting through uncertainty. *Journal of Teaching in Social Work, 26*(3/4), 167–179.

Askeland, G. A., & Payne, M. (2001). What is valid knowledge for social workers? *Social Work in Europe, 8*(3), 13–23.

Askeland, G. A., & Payne, M. (2001). Broadening the mind: Cross-national activities in social work. *European Journal of Social Work, 4* (3), 263–274.

The LICENSEE framework can help in preparing to move to a particular area of a country such as Canada (see for example Collins, Coleman, & Miller, 2002; DeAngelis & Monahan, 2008; Herrick & Stuart, 2005; Swain, 2001; and Turner, 1997) and Mexico (see Aguilar, 1997; Herrick & Stuart, 2005; and Zárate & Treviño, 2007).

Students and faculty interested in exploring the possibility of a practicum in another country will find the following two articles helpful:

Lough, B. J. (2009). Principles of effective practice in international social work field placements. *Journal of Social Work Education, 48*(3), 467–480.

Panos, P. T., Pettys, G. L, Cox, S. E., & Jones, E. (2004). Full survey of international field practicum placements of accredited schools of social work. *Journal of Social Work Education, 40*(3), 467–478.

CSWE will soon have a new publication available: *Guidebook for International Field Placements and Student Exchanges.* It will include a CD with sample forms and agreements that programs have used.

National Alliance on Mental Health (NAMI)

http://www.nami.org/
NAMI is a good example of a self-help group or network, describing itself as a grassroots advocacy organization. Its members include people who face mental health difficulties, their families, and their allies. It has both national and local offices, publishes the journal *Advocacy*, operates an information help line, and lobbies for legislation and policies to improve the lives of people affected by mental illness. NAMI representatives have proven to be staunch and effective advocates for effective regulation of social work and other health professions.

National Association of Black Social Workers (NABSW)

http://www.nabsw.org/mserver
In the words of its mission statement, NABSW is "committed to enhancing the quality of life and empowering people of African ancestry through advocacy, human services delivery, and research." This professional association grew out of the civil rights movement in the United States and has sustained both national and international leadership and local chapters with conferences, networking, research, scholarships, mentorship and other support for students, and influential position papers. Among the social work associations, NABSW has been most skeptical about licensure

and has effectively raised questions about the purpose and intended or actual outcomes of regulatory policies. Moreover, many members are licensed social workers and advocate strongly for the public protection of clients which licensing at its best affords. For example, at the local chapter conference in Minnesota on October 30, 2009, a panelist exhorted members to encourage their clients seeking mental health services to ask to see their service provider's license as one indicator of the provider's competence to help.

National Association of Deans and Directors of Schools of Social Work (NADD)

http://www.naddssw.org
Many of the MSW or social work doctoral programs in the United States are members of this association. It coordinates activities and initiatives with the other social work organizations here and globally. It holds annual meetings and an annual conference and cohosts or helps organize other national and international events, and it supports and is supported by CSWE. It was in response to a resolution from NADD that CSWE issued its position paper opposing mandatory licensing of social work faculty. Among the goals in the association's strategic plan is identifying and assessing trends with an accompanying action step to provide program offerings and dialogue opportunities on issues including licensing. NADD task forces focus on such areas as behavioral health, child welfare, gerontological social work, health disparities, international social work, the structure of social work education programs, and their response in times of trauma and disaster. The integral relationship between professional education and licensure results in many overlaps between the work of these task forces and issues of interest to regulators, including identification of minimum competencies, continuing education and training, assessment and evaluation, workforce development, and other emerging issues. As examples of the latter two concerns, the task force on the structure of programs is attending to the need for better title protection for social workers, and the task force responding to traumas and disasters facilitated the smooth transfer of students from the programs in New Orleans and other schools struck by hurricanes in 2005 while attendees at the NADD conference held in Texas that fall volunteered their social work services to evacuees from the communities that suffered devastation.

National Association of Social Workers (NASW)

http://www.socialworkers.org
NASW is the preeminent professional association for social workers in the

United States. Social work students are encouraged to join, and membership dues for students are significantly reduced. The NASW Code of Ethics expresses the fundamental values to which social workers commit themselves, and establishes a set of evolving standards to which professional social workers should aspire. The association publishes the *Encyclopedia of Social Work* (a good starting point for any research project related to licensing), professional journals such as *Social Work*, workforce studies, policy analyses, legislative updates, and many useful books. The association's website has been expanded and updated with useful information for the general public and a number of additional resources for members. For example, see the Student Starter Kit at http://www.socialworkers.org/students/starterKit.asp.

Under the caption *Licensing*, students will find this statement plus a link to ASWB's website:

A state social work license is . . .

- Issued to regulate the practice of social work
- Issued to protect the public
- Issued by and useful only in the jurisdiction (state) where the holder plans to practice.

A link to the NASW credentialing center is described as a resource for enhancing state licensure:http://www.socialworkers.org/credentials/default.asp.

Specialty certifications are available for both BSW and MSW practitioners.

Each state chapter of NASW is also a good resource for information and advocacy on local regulatory issues and policies, and students can link to their chapter through the national NASW office or website. NASW members have access to more resources, including the informative "Legal Issue of the Month" feature. For example, the article for the month of May 2009 was "Social Work Supervision for State Licensure." The site can be confusing to search, though improvements are being made.

NASW Press also publishes many texts, such as Rosenfeld, L. B., Gaye, J. S., Ayalon, O., & Lahad, M. (2005). *When their world falls apart: Helping families and children manage the effects of disasters.* Washington, DC: NASW Press.

National Network of Social Work Managers

https://www.socialworkmanager.org/
This association of social workers who are administrators in a wide range

of nonprofit, for-profit, and government agencies is a good resource for information and networking. It publishes a leading social work journal in administration and supervision, *Administration in Social Work*, and it also has set up standards and a credential for social work administrators as a certified social work manager through its Academy of Social Work Managers.

Social Work Today

www.socialworktoday.com
This bi-monthly journal covers news and topics relevant to social work standards, ethics, careers, and regulation of practice; updates on licensing frequently appear in a popular readable format.

Index

Note: Page numbers followed by "f" or "t" refer to figures or tables respectively.